SACRAMENTO PUBLIC LIBRARY
828 "I" Street
Sacramento, CA 95814
10/14

DAY OF THE DEAD CRAFTS

MORE THAN 24 PROJECTS THAT CELEBRATE DÍA DE LOS MUERTOS

Senior Acquisitions Editor
Roxane Cerda

Executive Editor
Kerry Arquette

Editor
Darlene D'Agostino

Art Direction & Design
Andrea Zocchi

Copy Editor
Dena Twinem

Unless noted all photographs are © 2008 by Andrea Zocchi

wiley.com

Day of the Dead Crafts:
More than 24 Projects that Celebrate Día de los Muertos

Copyright © 2008 by Cantata Books, Inc. (www.cantatabooks.com)

Published by Wiley Publishing, Inc., Hoboken, New Jersey

No part of this publication may be reproduced, stored in a retrieval system or transmitted in any form or by any means, electronic, mechanical, photocopying, recording, scanning or otherwise, except as permitted under Sections 107 or 108 of the 1976 United States Copyright Act, without either the prior written permission of the Publisher, or authorization through payment of the appropriate per-copy fee to the Copyright Clearance Center, 222 Rosewood Drive, Danvers, MA 01923, (978) 750-8400, fax (978) 646-8600, or on the web at www.copyright.com. Requests to the Publisher for permission should be addressed to the Legal Department, Wiley Publishing, Inc., 10475 Crosspoint Blvd., Indianapolis, IN 46256, (317) 572-3447, fax (317) 572-4355, or online at http://www.wiley.com/go/permissions.

Wiley, the Wiley Publishing logo, and related trademarks are trademarks or registered trademarks of John Wiley & Sons, Inc. and/or its affiliates. All other trademarks are the property of their respective owners. Wiley Publishing, Inc. is not associated with any product or vendor mentioned in this book.

The publisher and the author make no representations or warranties with respect to the accuracy or completeness of the contents of this work and specifically disclaim all warranties, including without limitation warranties of fitness for a particular purpose. No warranty may be created or extended by sales or promotional materials. The advice and strategies contained herein may not be suitable for every situation. This work is sold with the understanding that the publisher is not engaged in rendering legal, accounting, or other professional services. If professional assistance is required, the services of a competent professional person should be sought. Neither the publisher nor the author shall be liable for damages arising here from. The fact that an organization or Website is referred to in this work as a citation and/or a potential source of further information does not mean that the author or the publisher endorses the information the organization or Website may provide or recommendations it may make. Further, readers should be aware that Internet Websites listed in this work may have changed or disappeared between when this work was written and when it is read.

For general information on our other products and services or to obtain technical support please contact our Customer Care Department within the U.S. at (800) 762-2974, outside the U.S. at (317) 572-3993 or fax (317) 572-4002.

Wiley also publishes its books in a variety of electronic formats. Some content that appears in print may not be available in electronic books. For more information about Wiley products, please visit our web site at www.wiley.com.

Library of Congress Cataloging-in-Publication Data available from the publisher upon request.

Printed in China

10—9—8—7—6—5—4

DAY OF THE DEAD CRAFTS

MORE THAN 24 PROJECTS THAT CELEBRATE DÍA DE LOS MUERTOS

Jerry Vigil, Kerry Arquette & Andrea Zocchi

cantata|books

www.cantatabooks.com

INTRODUCTION

There is nothing pretentious about folk art, and that's exactly where its charm lies. Unlike fine art, the folk variety is usually created by untrained artists and crafters. Whether their artwork is simplistic or more complex, it reflects the culture, customs, and beliefs of the society in which they live and with which they identify. Folk art is the everyman's view of life—his own and the lives of those around him. Without being impacted by rules imposed upon artists who are classically trained, the folk artist simply "makes it the way he sees it." While folk art may be raw, it is also honest.

Whether you have crafted before or are new to the hobby, you'll find creating Day of the Dead folk art an exciting and fulfilling experience. Just as there are no mandates as to how the Day of the Dead must be observed, there are no "musts" when it comes to the artwork that is associated with the holiday. As you turn the pages of this book, you'll discover a wide variety of visions and styles. In fact, no two artists make identical pieces. Your Day of the Dead artwork will be just as unique.

Within this book you'll find inspiration in work created by some of the best-loved Day of the Dead artists in the country. Techniques for dozens of projects are stepped out with illustrative photos, making it easy for you to re-create elements. You'll find interesting sidebars that will deepen your understanding of the Day of the Dead, its history and traditions.

Folk art can be utilitarian. It can be decorative. In some cases, it is both. Day of the Dead art often crosses the line. Calaveras, masks, decorative skulls, jewelry, and other traditional elements easily travel from a holiday altar to a display case or living room wall. We hope you will find ways to display and enjoy your creations year-round.

TABLE OF CONTENTS

THE HISTORY OF THE DAY OF THE DEAD

More than 3,000 years ago, the Aztec Indians, who dwelled in Mexico, spent four months each year honoring and tending to their dead with ceremonies and rituals. The Spanish conquistadors who arrived in Mexico in the 16th century tried to eradicate the established traditions associated with the holiday, replacing them with practices associated with and condoned by the Roman Catholic Church. Rather than turn their backs on their history, the indigenous people chose to meld ancient traditions with those of the church.

Aztec dancers await their chance to perform at the Hollywood Forever Cemetery.

Papel picados, decoratively cut paper banners, flutter above the Olvera Street plaza.

Artist: Unknown, A colorful ofrenda, or Day of the Dead altar, stands at the Hollywood Forever Cemetery.

A display of calaveras draws customers to The Folk Tree, a popular California craft store and gallery.

Day of the Dead artist Cesco (Frank Pamies) holds a skull he created for The Festival de la Gente.

Although activities associated with the Day of the Dead continue to evolve, the purpose behind the celebration remains constant: The holiday allows families to dedicate time each year to honor those who have passed away. For those who actively celebrate the Day of the Dead, remembering the deceased is more than an act of fondness; it is an obligation of respect. Observance of the Day of the Dead ensures that a beloved's soul will never be forgotten and therefore truly will never die. Many participants believe that a person can experience three deaths. The first death is the expiration of the body. The second death occurs when the body is laid to rest. The third and final death takes place only if and when the departed is forgotten.

Traditional dancers perform at Day of the Dead festivities at the Hollywood Forever Cemetery.

A custom-painted car with a Day of the Dead theme at the Hollywood Forever Cemetery.

Each year the Day of the Dead is celebrated in cities, towns, and villages throughout Mexico on November 1 and 2. People attend mass, set up altars in their homes, and clean and decorate the graves of family members. They gather in cemeteries for picnics, dancing, and singing while reconnecting with their roots. Children play with skeleton marionettes. Restaurants and bakery windows are decorated with gaily painted skeleton figures eating the treats associated with the holiday—sugar skulls and *pan de los muertos*, a sweet bread that is often topped with colorful icing. Towns, big and small, now fill with American tourists drawn to Mexico to witness and take part in the celebrations.

Here in the United States, more and more communities are developing an interest in the holiday. Stores are stocked with Day of the Dead art, sugar skull molds, and coloring books. Streets are gaily decorated with festive cut-paper banners. In San Francisco, hoards paint their faces into skeleton grins and parade past altars

along a designated route. Chicago art galleries host special Day of the Dead exhibits showcasing some of the world's most talented folk artists. Los Angeles holds a variety of celebrations, the most popular being an event held at the Hollywood Forever Cemetery. There, people from across the country and Mexico build elaborate altars. Crafters sell their work while dancers and singers entertain the thousands who attend. The festival is a joyful party that celebrates the lives of those who have moved on while mocking death's power to take from us the most important aspect of life— the relationship we have with those we love.

When death is greeted warmly and with good humor, it no longer clutches us in a grip of fear. The Day of the Dead is as much a celebration of life as it is a call to those who have passed to return and enjoy a holiday in their honor.

Wooden sculptures by artist Chad Mora fill a booth at the Hollywood Forever Cemetery.

GLOSSARY OF TERMS

Calavera Whimsical one- or two-dimensional skeleton figures
Catrina (Katrina) Female aristocratic calaveras
Kahlo, Frida (1907-1954) Mexican painter best known for her colorful self-portraits
Ofrenda Altars set up to welcome and honor the dead
Pan de los muertos Sweet bread eaten during the holiday
Papel picados Cut paper banners used to decorate altars
Posada, Jose Guadalupe (1852-1913) Celebrated Mexican artist best known for his calavera drawings
Sugar skulls Decorative molded skulls set on altars and eaten
Virgin of Guadalupe Mexican icon depicting the apparition of the Virgin Mary

OFRENDAS

Altars to Welcome Returning Souls

It is a long journey from the afterworld to the earthly homes where loved ones still live. But on the Day of the Dead, souls who make the trip find a warm welcome awaiting them. Observant families spend days preparing meaningful ofrendas, or altars, within their homes to honor those returning and assure their comfort. The ofrendas are stocked with food, drink, and most anything else the souls might need to enjoy their visit.

Ideally ofrendas are placed in the hub of the house. From the time souls are called back to earth by the ringing of church bells, fireworks, or prayer, to the moment of departure, they are surrounded by the lively chatter and gossip of family members. The ofrenda remains in place throughout the holiday.

Some ofrendas are dismantled after the Day of the Dead, but many artists display their altars year-round. These emotionally moving pieces of art provide a showcase for smaller pieces such as calaveras, nichos, masks, skulls, and flowers.

Artist: Unknown, Lakewood Cultural Center

WHAT IS YOUR OFRENDA STYLE?

Altars are, without a doubt, the most spectacular craft project associated with the Day of the Dead. Artists who make them love the creative possibilities they offer. Should their ofrenda be large or small? elaborate or simple? modern or traditional? Will it hang on a wall or extend across a large area? Will it be displayed inside or outside? Before you begin to craft your own ofrenda, be ready to answer those questions. Each type of ofrenda boasts its own type of beauty.

Artist: Cal Duran, Lakewood Cultural Center

Artist: Monica Gomez, The Folk Tree

Artist: Cal Duran, Lakewood Cultural Center

Sleek and Minimalist

Tented fabric creates a canopy for a stunning ofrenda consisting of a painted image and a lace-covered pedestal. The ofrenda requires a high ceiling and an expanse of uncluttered space to fit the fabric, bench, and potted flowers.

Simple and Rustic

A worn wooden table and woven blankets provide a base for this simple ofrenda that can be displayed in a small corner of a room. White tower candles, flowers, bread, cactus, and a photo are used to decorate the altar.

Compact and Ornate

An ofrenda that hangs on the wall can be displayed in any room in the home. This altar includes a gameboard background, a nicho, or niche, skeletons, a photo, and a variety of decorative embellishments.

Large and Complex

This ofrenda honors generations of mothers and grandmothers and includes many photos. Statues, nichos, flowers, candles, baskets, fruit, bread, and much more fill the entire corner of an art gallery.

Artists: Ofelia Esparza, Xavier Esparza, Denise Esparza-Carrillo, Pico House Gallery

PREPARE AN OFRENDA

Your ofrenda is as personal and unique as those whom it honors. There are no "musts" in the construction of the altar or the elements set upon it. However, more traditional ofrendas are built on three levels to represent the three forms of death: the death of the body, the burial, and being forgotten by those left behind. Items placed upon these altars are symbolically meaningful and steeped in history.

Decorations

Decoratively cut paper banners called papel picados adorn the ofrenda and remind us of the fragility of life. They represent the element of air. Skulls and calaveras, or skeleton figures, mock death. Images of saints, written prayers, and pieces of artwork also have a place on the altar.

Candles and Incense

Four candles are placed on the top level of the ofrenda to represent the cardinal directions and the element of fire. Additional candles are lit for each returning soul, while an extra burns for the forgotten one. Incense cleanses the air of negative energy and guides returning souls home.

Photos

Images of loved ones are set on the highest level of the ofrenda to honor their physical form. More than one photo may appear on the altar depending upon the number of souls being hosted.

Personal Possessions

Favorite possessions that belonged to the departed are displayed on the altar so that the souls can once again enjoy them. Common items might include books, jewelry, hobbies, scrapbooks, a Bible, and keepsakes.

Wash Basin and Toiletries

Souls are provided the opportunity to freshen up after their long journey so that they may be comfortable during their stay.

Food and Drink

The element of water and other favored forms of beverage are included on the ofrenda to quench the souls' thirst. Pan de muertos, a decorated loaf of sweet bread, fruits, vegetables, and other foods represent the element of earth. The returning souls enjoy feeding on their essence. Decorative sugar skulls add sweetness to the Day of the Dead celebrations while salt purifies and seasons it.

Artist: Jerry Vigil

OPTIONAL EXTRAS

Beyond the traditional elements found on ofrendas, artists may choose to embellish their altars in a variety of ways. They include twinkling lights, poems, albums, awards, and other elements that add to the personal nature of the artwork. More recently, some artists have even set monitors or television sets on the altar in order to play DVDs of the departed and happy times they have shared. Extras can be added over time as you continue to develop your vision for your work.

Statement of Purpose

A short message about the meaning and creation of an ofrenda allows viewers to better interpret some of the symbolic pieces included on the altar. It also calls attention to specific details that might otherwise be overlooked. The statement may invite visitors to participate in the honoring.

...This "Abuela" is Grandmother Time, spewing forth the cycle of Life, with a glint of death in her eye, watching bud turn to blossom, petals dropping, ultimately fading away—all a metaphor for this life of ours. As an altar, I have asked the visitor to participate by throwing seed into the cauldron as an act of remembering the loss of a loved one, and to also remember one's own death—Memento Mori.
Matt De Haven

Artist: Matt De Haven, The Folk Tree

Artist: Unknown, Hollywood Forever Cemetery

Lights

Ofrendas that will be viewed in the dark take on a different feeling when illuminated with candles, holiday lights, or *luminarias*. Many artists combine a variety of lights to take advantage of their different colors and intensities. The placement of the lights call attention to specific portions of the ofrenda, bathing them while allowing other sections to fall into shadow. These photos (above) show how one ofrenda can take on an entirely different personality when lit by daylight versus incandescent Christmas lights.

Artist: Unknown, Festival de la Gente

Biography and Personal Information

For viewers less familiar with the deceased, an altar is more meaningful if they know a bit about the life of the one honored. Including a short history that cites birth date and day of passing, where the deceased grew up, and major accomplishments during his or her life enriches the ofrenda. The personal information might also tell a short story that speaks to the character or personality of the departed.

OFRENDA THEMES

Ofrendas may honor a single loved one or a group of family members. They may also focus on a group of people who are tied together in a special way, whether it was a shared pleasure such as a hobby, or a tragic and untimely death such as 9/11. Artists also create ofrendas to call attention to social causes such as war, poverty, drug abuse, or the need for better education. An ofrenda can tell the world that you care.

Honoring Surfers and Water Lovers

Photos of professional and amateur surfers are featured on this ofrenda honoring water lovers who believed in the utopia of the ocean and spent much of their lives enjoying it. The images are displayed on a watercolored background and inside a tub. Red candles and flowers contribute to the design.

Artist: R. Taylor, Festival de la Gente

Celebrating Musicians and Dancers

A porcelain dancing couple, merry calaveras engaged in dancing, singing, and music-making, as well as beautiful musical instruments, papel picados, flowers, and photos are found throughout this ofrenda. It honors the rich arts community of Veracruz, Mexico, home to the artist's grandparents who were responsible for passing on their love of music to the family's younger generations.

Artist: Gonzoles, Hollywood Forever Cemetery

Artist: Rita Almanza, The Folk Tree

Altar for Peace

An illuminated peace symbol tops this ofrenda. Photos of loved ones, personal possessions, and calaveras support the main element in the display—a large box filled with sand and toy soldiers. Visitors are asked to write the name of a soldier who has died on a slip of paper and place it in the sand as a sign of honor.

Artist: Unknown, Hollywood Forever Cemetery

Remembering a Celebrity

Frida Kahlo, a beloved Mexican painter, is honored on this large ofrenda. The painted image of Frida heads the altar. A large heart-shaped pillow, photos, catrinas, and books spread across a colorful rug and stairs.

A Stand Against Drugs

When a friend dies of a drug habit, loved ones are left to wonder "why?" The artist who created this ofrenda pulls no punches. He remembers and commemorates the life of a good friend but at the same time he holds a torch to the ugly and useless cause of his early death.

Artist: Cal Duran, Lakewood Cultural Center

CREATE A UNIQUE MEMORIAL

The top portion of an ofrenda, the memorial, is the focal point of the altar. Traditionally, this is where the photo of the deceased resides surrounded by flowers and candles. You can create a memorial using many craft supplies you may already have around your home. Here is just one example.

SUPPLIES

- Foam board
- White paper
- Craft glue
- Tissue paper
- Decoupage medium
- Cigar box
- Acrylic paint
- Virgin of Guadalupe stamp
- Clear embossing ink
- Clear embossing powder
- Red spray dye
- Metallic gold dye
- Embossing heat tool
- Burning heart stamp
- 2 small tin cans
- Sheet adhesive
- Gold pipe cleaner
- Painted sugar skull die cut
- Heirloom photo
- Silk flowers

Artist: Erikia Ghumm

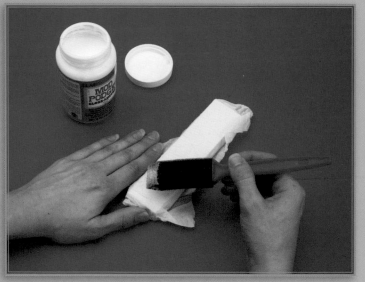

Step 1

Cut one 3 x 12" piece of foam board to form the base of your memorial. Cut two 1 ½ x 6" pieces of foam board to form the top of the memorial. Cut the starburst decoration for the top of the memorial from foam board. Glue the smaller strips together and allow them to dry overnight weighed down with heavy books.

Step 2

Crumple tissue paper and apply it to all of the foam-board pieces with decoupage medium.

HONORING THE ANIMA SOLA

The lone soul is one who has no family left on earth to remember and honor him. The responsibility of welcoming this soul back for Day of the Dead falls on the community in which he lived. For this reason, members of towns big and small work together to create an ofrenda that honors all the lone souls who have passed. It is a group memorial that keeps the lone souls from passing forever into the Beyond without the opportunity to return again.

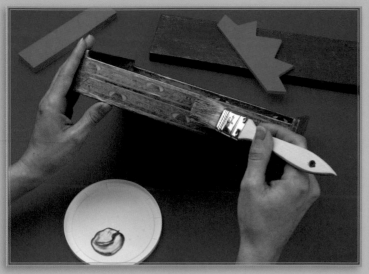

Step 3

Remove and discard the lid from a cigar box. Paint the inside of the cigar box, the foam-board pieces, and the sunburst with acrylic paint and allow to dry. Apply a wash of metallic antique brass paint to all except the starburst pieces. Allow to dry.

Step 4

Stamp the Virgin of Guadalupe image onto white paper using clear embossing ink. Sprinkle the image with clear embossing powder and apply heat with an embossing heat tool.

Step 5

Spray the stamped image with red dye. Allow to dry. Spray the image again with metallic gold dye. Repeat steps 4 and 5 to create a second stamped Virgin of Guadalupe design. Use a burning heart stamp to create a single burning heart image by following Steps 4 and 5.

Step 6

Trim the edges of the Virgin of Guadalupe images. Silhouette cut the burning heart image. Apply the Virgin of Guadalupe images to small tin cans with sheet adhesive. Glue the burning heart to the center of the foam-board sunburst.

Step 7
Glue all of the pieces together and allow to dry overnight.

Step 8
Embellish the altar with gold pipe cleaners, a painted sugar skull die cut, a photo, and silk marigolds.

WHO WAS THE VIRGIN OF GUADALUPE?

In early December 1531, on a hill near Mexico City, Juan Diego Cuauhtlatoatzin reported seeing an apparition of the Virgin Mary. The Spanish bishop demanded proof of Diego's claim. And so, Diego returned to the hill to collect roses, although they would not normally have been in bloom, and presented them to the bishop. The roses, it is said, left the appearance of the Virgin on the cloth in which Diego carried them. News of the appearance of "*La Virgen Morena*" (The Brown-Skinned Virgin) swept across the country. Also known as Our Lady of Guadalupe and the Virgin of Guadalupe, the icon grew to become the most beloved religious and cultural image of the people. Today, the Virgin of Guadalupe's feast day is celebrated on December 12.

Artist: Jerry Vigil

Calaveras

Skeletons With Personality

Skeletons play an important role in Day of the Dead observances. While some cultures associate the bony figures with scary things that go bump in the night, others, including Mexican and Latino communities that regularly celebrate Day of the Dead, consider them far less threatening. Skeletons, or calaveras, take up residence everywhere between late October and early November. Their painted grins beckon customers from storefront windows, decorate public parks and museums, adorn ofrendas, and are collected by eager tourists.

Calaveras prance and dance, mocking death and inviting the living to do the same. Their message seems to be "Death's no big deal, and you have no reason to fear it." Many calaveras satirize the human existence and tickle us into re-examining our serious notions of our pedestrian tasks and our existence.

Artist: Jerry Vigil

Clay Calaveras Span the Spectrum

The majority of calaveras are made from some type of clay, but that seems to be all that the skeleton figures have in common. A clay calavera may be so charmingly primitive that you have to look twice before realizing it truly is a skeleton, or so complex that you are rendered speechless at the patience of the artist. While a calavera depicts the personality of the character upon which it is modeled, it may speak just as loudly about the personality of the artist. Because calaveras are satirical figures, they are the artist's commentary about people, places, and situations he or she deals with on a daily basis. No two artists are alike, and you would be hard-pressed to find two similar calaveras.

Artist: Jody Travous Nee

Artist: Kerry Arquette

Small and Simple Equals Endearing

"When I lived in Florida, I was too inhibited to go to Playalindz Beach, the local nude beach," says artist Jody Travous Nee. Years later, she let this uninhibited calavera (above) experience the sun and sand instead. Only 3" tall, this polymer clay, hand-painted calavera catches some rays while posing on the beach—a wooden disk covered with sandpaper.

Expansive Sets Up a Scenario

"There are 'shoe gals' and 'purse gals,' but Aunt Carmen loved her hats!" says artist Kerry Arquette. "As a child I couldn't wait to go over to her house so that I could play dress-up with them." This stylish calavera (right) on top of a spray-painted hatbox was made to honor Aunt Carmen. The calavera and hats were made of polymer clay and then painstakingly painted.

Artist: Jerry Vigil

Artist: Jerry Vigil

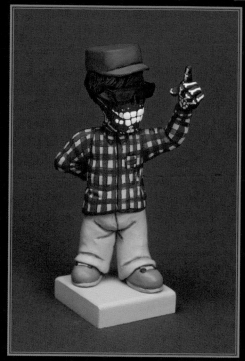

Artist: Jerry Vigil

Signature Styles and Palettes Define an Artist

"I use cobalt blue on my calaveras as a unique signature. It's common to use white on the artwork, but if it is blue, chances are it's mine," says artist Jerry Vigil. Vigil's blue calaveras have bigger-than-life personalities. From homeboy gear to zoot suit, these posturing calaveras are confident that they are making a fashion statement in their detailed outfits.

FROM THE ARTIST: JERRY VIGIL

"El Día de los Muertos is a cultural celebration that is growing larger and larger each year. It functions as a wonderful teaching tool and a format to understand the Latino community. The celebration exists in both the traditional sense and in the contemporary. It is important to me to celebrate this occasion with art as a way to bridge the traditional art into the contemporary art so the cultural meaning is not lost. I became interested in the art of El Día de los Muertos as a way to educate myself on the culture of my *familia* and to celebrate them. If you remember someone, they will never truly die."

Artist: Jerry Vigil

WHO WILL YOUR CALAVERA BE?

Before you can "create," you need to settle on a persona for your skeleton. The task can seem daunting. Where do you begin? Unlike some artwork that calls for you to look inward for inspiration, your best calavera ideas may be right outside your door. Take a walk and note the outlandish personalities around you. Pick up a newspaper to see what's going on in your community. Flip to the comics for a giggle. Dive into a stack of magazines, go to a movie, or turn on the tube. Root through old photos. (Yearbooks provide terrific fodder for ideas.) Think about your friends and relatives. Next, pretend you are a comedy writer whose mission it is to satirize, or poke good-humored fun at, a personality or situation. Imagine what it would be like to draw a caricature of the person you plan to create. If you wish, sketch the concepts and then pull out your clay. Let the good times roll.

The Gang at the Neighborhood Hangout

There is no place like a salon to really let your hair down. Strangers find themselves chatting about all kinds of things while under the dryer or enveloped in a mist of spray. Local ice cream parlors, arcades, bars, and the mall also provide great people-watching opportunities. Take along a camera and covertly snap photos of interesting characters.

Artist: Tamra Kohl

Artist: Tamra Kohl

A Rare Relative

Every family has an eccentric character whose life reads like a novel. He may be a heroic figure who talks about his dashing deeds, a practical joker who shares his best "gotcha's," or one of those special people who turns heads wearing his favorite fashion from many years ago. Capture the traits that make him colorful in a calavera.

Creatures With Claws

Whether you are a cat person, a dog person, or prefer creatures with hoofs, feathers, or scales, chances are there is a special animal in your life. Capture the sweet, sassy, and sometimes naughty personality of your pet in a calavera that shows it enjoying life at its fullest.

Artist: Andrea Zocchi

Artist: Tamra Kohl

A News Event

Sometimes ya just gotta wonder what those crooks were thinking! You know the ones: They rob a bank and leave a trail of money leading to their hideout, or they accidentally shut themselves in their car trunk while stashing the ill-gotten goods. Create a calavera to commemorate crooks who should have chosen another profession.

Clay Calavera

You can create a calavera in less than an hour using oven-bake clay and acrylic paint. The key to success is in keeping your first attempt simple. As you advance in the art, you may wish to add more details to your figure.

Sculpting a Basic Skeleton Form

A skeleton figure can be complex or fairly simple. You may choose to carefully form each limb, trying to replicate the major bones in, for example, the leg or rib cage. Or you may decide to make a more free-form shape and paint on the details after baking. The choice is up to you; both approaches can provide wonderful effects. In order to access both possibilities, you need to first master the creation of a basic skeleton shape.

Supplies

- 4-6 ounces polymer clay
- Several gauges of thin, flexible armature wire
- Wire cutters
- Clay tools for cutting, shaping, and detailing
- Gesso (acrylic primer)
- Acrylic paints or acrylic paint pens
- Fine-tipped paintbrushes

Try This

For sculpting tools, try bamboo skewers, a school compass, a craft knife, flatware, sewing tools and supplies such as a seam ripper and large spools, as well as nails and pins.

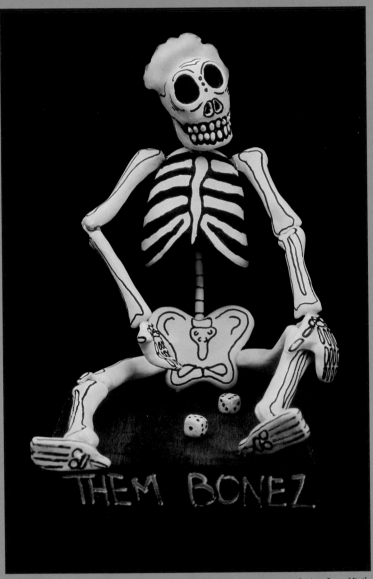

Artist: Jerry Vigil

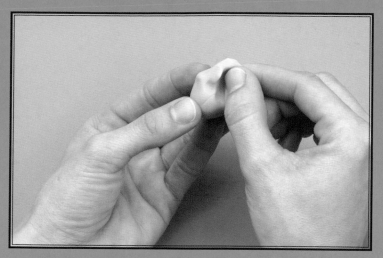

Step 1

Form a head for your calavera by rolling a piece of polymer clay into a ball. To form the jaw, use your thumb to pinch the back lower half of the skull. Continue until you've created a square jaw line with a flat chin. Manipulate the upper portion of the ball until you are satisfied with the shape of the head.

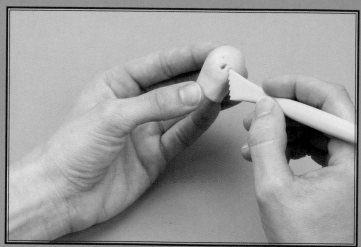

Step 2

Use a fine-tipped sculpting tool to gently press into the clay head, creating small slash shapes for the nose.

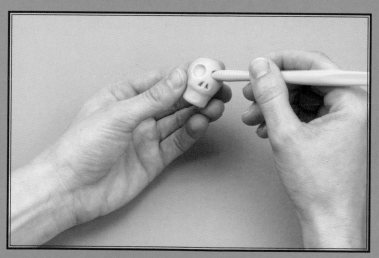

Step 3

Use a rounded sculpting tool to press eyes into your clay head. Because the size and placement of the eyes will largely determine the personality of your calavera, you may wish to sketch your concept on paper before beginning to implement your ideas on clay.

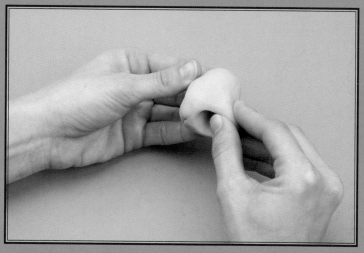

Step 4

Create the rib cage by forming a teardrop shape out of clay. Flatten the top of the teardrop (the portion upon which the skull will sit). To hollow out the rib cage, insert your thumb into the base of the shape and pinch out the center.

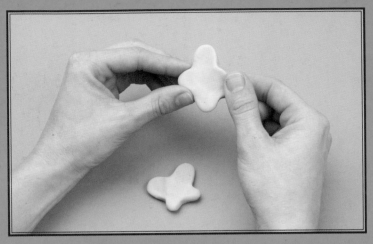

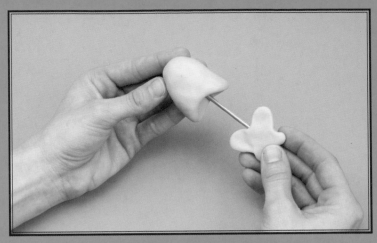

Step 5

For the pelvis, pinch a single flat butterfly shape out of a piece of clay.

Step 6

Connect the rib cage to the pelvis by inserting a piece of sturdy armature wire through the lower portion of the rib cage and the top portion of the pelvis. Do not press the two clay sections completely together. Instead, leave a section of exposed wire to create the spine.

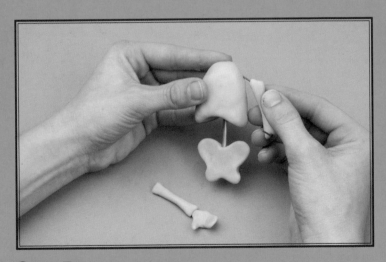

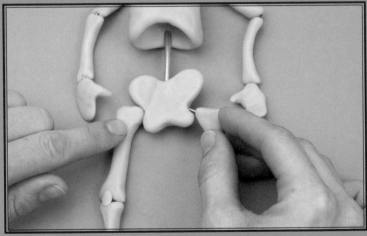

Step 7

Form upper and lower sections of the arms by rolling clay into narrow tube shapes. Pinch small pieces of clay to form hands. Connect the lower arm and the hand pieces with thin pieces of armature wire. Press the upper arm section into the rib cage. Connect the lower arm/hand section to the upper arm piece using wire.

Step 8

Form the legs in the same manner as you have formed the arms. Attach all the pieces with thin pieces of armature wire. Use wire to add the head on top of the rib cage. Place your calavera on a cookie sheet. Pose it by gently manipulating the body parts. Because of the wire "joints," you will be able to do some manipulating after the figure has been baked, but major positioning should be done before baking. Bake according to manufacturer's directions.

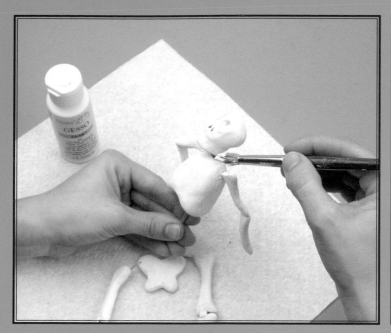 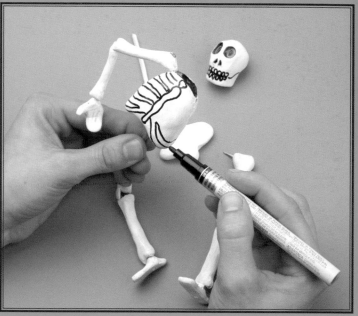

Step 9

Remove the calavera from the oven and allow it to cool. Paint it with a coat of Gesso. Repeat, if desired.

Step 10

Complete your calavera by detailing the bones. Here, the negative spaces around the bones are painted with a black acrylic paint pen. Detail the face by painting in the eyes, nose, and drawing on a mouth.

A CALAVERA OF CORRECT PROPORTIONS

When creating the pieces of your calavera, the ratios below will help you proportion the body parts. Notice that these measurements are relative to the size of the skull of your figure, so create the skull before working on other body parts.

Height: The human figure is an average of 7 heads high.

Torso: The distance from the top of the head to the bottom of the chest is 2 heads.

Buttocks: The length from top to bottom of the buttocks is 1 head.

Leg length: The distance from the hip to the toes is 4 heads.

Wingspan: The width from shoulder to shoulder is 3 heads.

Forearm: The distance from the elbow to the end of outstretched fingers is 2 heads.

Girth of hand: The distance from the wrist to the end of the outstretched fingers of the hand is 1 head.

DRESSED MALE CALAVERA

Some artists like to make the skeleton figure for a calavera and then dress it in clay clothing. Others feel it is easier to forgo the process of creating the skeleton form, and simply make a dressed figure. Molding a dressed calavera and then painting exposed body parts to look like bones takes less time than the two-step process of making and then dressing your figure. The results are virtually the same.

 ## SUPPLIES

- 4-6 ounces polymer clay
- Several gauges of thin, flexible armature wire
- Wire cutters
- Clay tools for rolling, cutting, shaping, and detailing
- Gesso (acrylic primer)
- Acrylic paints or acrylic paint pens
- Fine-tipped paintbrushes

 ## TRY THIS

If painting intimidates you, create clothing for your calavera using colored polymer clay. No painting necessary!

Artist: Jerry Vigil

Step 1

Create the male calavera's skull as you created the skull for your basic skeleton according to the directions on page 35. Pinch out the clay to form the jaw and press in the clay to form eyes and a nose.

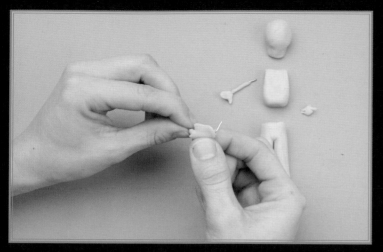

Step 2

Create each piece of clothing. Mold a teardrop-shaped shirt, two sleeve shapes, pants, and shoes. Make arms by wrapping a thin layer of clay around two pieces of thin armature wire. Attach molded hands to the ends of the clay-covered wire. Connect the pieces of your calavera using thin pieces of armature wire as shown on page 36.

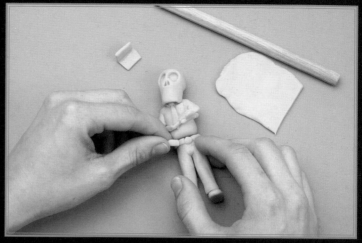

Step 3

Detail by adding a belt cut from a thin piece of rolled clay. Create a pocket, tie, and laptop computer (or other accessories) in a similar manner.

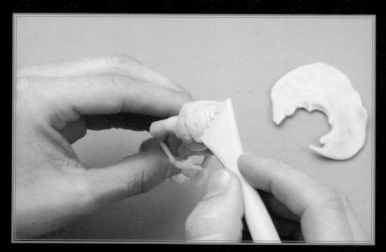

Step 4

Roll out a thin layer of clay. Cut a "toupee" shape. Gently press the hair portion in place. Use the side of a clay tool to style the hair, creating waves and a part.

Step 5

Position your calavera with the computer, or other accessories, in his hands. Bake according to manufacturer's directions. Allow to cool and then paint.

Dressed Female Calavera

Female calaveras are created in much the same way as male figures, however you'll need to spend time adding some alluring curves to the torso of a lovely lady's body. Perhaps the most fun part of working on a female calavera is making her hair. The style you select—whether it is a back-combed bob, pigtails, or Rapunzel locks, will define her personality as much as her expression or clothing.

 ## Supplies

- 4-6 ounces polymer clay
- Extruder
- Several grades of thin, flexible armature wire
- Wire cutters
- Clay tools for rolling, cutting, shaping, and detailing
- Gesso (acrylic primer)
- Acrylic paints or acrylic paint pens
- Fine-tipped paintbrushes

 ## Try This

Use a variety of paint finishes to make your calavera even more interesting. Try matte for your calavera's skin and glossy for the clothing or hair.

Artist: Jerry Vigil

Step 1

Create the female calavera's skull as you created the skull for your basic skeleton (see page 35). Make hair by forcing clay through a polymer-clay extruder.

Step 2

Use a wedge-shaped clay tool to cut the clay away from the extruder.

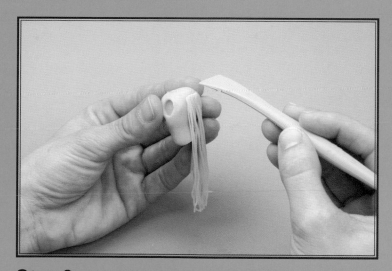

Step 3

Attach strands of hair to the skull by pressing the ends gently into the clay using a flat-edged tool. Begin at a low point along the neckline.

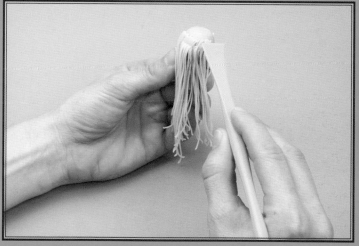

Step 4

Continue to add layers of extruded hair, working upward from the neckline, until the entire scalp portion has been covered.

Step 5

Turn the skull upside down, allowing the hair to drape.

Step 6

Begin to gently twist the hair into a cone. Turn the skull upright and pile the twisted hair into a swirled beehive hairdo.

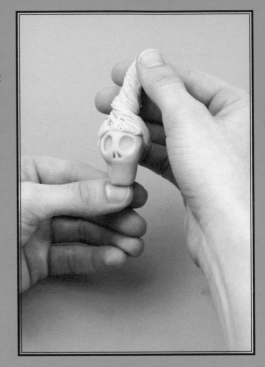

TRY THIS

Have fun creating your own hairstyles for your female calaveras. Give them a full-blown bouffant, braid the hair, or make it curl.

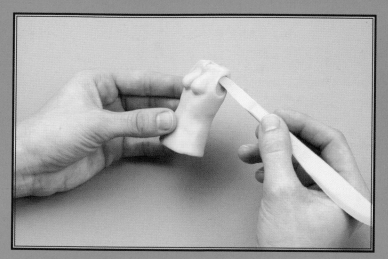

Step 7

Use clay to form a dress-shaped torso. Apply teardrop-shaped pieces of clay for breasts. Smooth the seams with your fingertips or a rounded sculpting tool. Create indentations for the sleeves and neck.

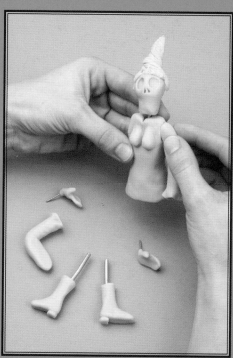

Step 8

Form hands, sleeves, and boots. Connect all of the clay pieces with small pieces of armature wires (see page 36). Bake according to manufacturer's directions. Allow to cool, and paint as desired.

DEALING WITH DISASTERS

Polymer clay is very workable, even after it has been baked. It can be sanded, filed, carved, drilled, cut with a band saw, filled with spackle, and scraped with various tools. So when your baked piece has issues, don't panic. Just fix it!

- **Problem:** The calavera is covered with fingerprints. **Fix:** Scrape the offending area with the flat of a razor blade.
- **Problem:** The calavera loses an arm/leg in baking. **Fix:** Drill small holes into the broken piece and the portion from which it had previously been attached. Insert a small-gauge wire into the holes to reconnect the pieces. Glue.
- **Problem:** The calavera is overbaked and turns black. **Fix:** Paint multiple coats of Gesso to cover the darkened polymer clay before painting with your acrylics.
- **Problem:** An arm/leg moved during baking and needs to be repositioned. **Fix:** Saw off the appendage at a convenient joint and drill a hole for small-gauge wire. Bend the wire to the needed angle and insert it into the joint. Glue.
- **Problem:** The calavera keeps dropping the object I want it to hold. **Fix:** Use a polymer super glue to attach the piece.

Detailed Male Calavera

Wire, metal, beads, baubles, fiber, fabric, and other materials can add texture, dimension, and bit of glitz to your clay calavera. Use other products to create everything from funky hair to jewelry. You may add metal elements prior to baking your polymer clay, but save the other heat-sensitive embellishments until after your clay has been baked and cooled. Be careful of the proportion of supplies you select. Remember that, while big on personality, your calavera may be smaller in stature than you realize.

Hair

This cool dude's hair more than just looks wiry. It IS wiry! To create his do, short pieces of wire were cut, pressed into the clay skull, and then painted.

Shirt

A soft blue felt strip runs down the center of this polymer clay shirt. The same blue fabric forms a pocket. The pocket and the shirt sport shiny buttons made of seed pearls.

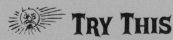 **Try This**

Go on a scavenger hunt! Your garage, sewing box, odds-and-ends drawers, and medicine cabinet hold treasures perfect for detailing your calavera. With a bit of creativity, costume jewelry, wire, fasteners, and even brush bristles can all be used to give your calavera his own special style.

Belt and Shoes

Real leather soles and leather laces ensure that these shoes will last until he outgrows them. Leather was used to create his belt, and wire forms a buckle.

Bling

No really cool guy hits the town without an earring or two, or three. This dude's wearing an earring made out of gold wire. A gold chain loops from his pants pocket.

Artist: Tamra Kohl

Detailed Female Calavera

Dressing up your lady calavera is as much fun as combining fashion design with an afternoon of doll play. You are in charge of the colors and textures she wears. And, by integrating things that sparkle into your concept, you can turn a plain clay calavera into something very ooh la la.

Hair and Eyelashes

This lovely's hair is made of fluffy pipe cleaners that were secured to the skull with glue after the figure had been baked.

The ribbon headband sports a bright red silk rose. Black wire was used to create the unbelievably long eyelashes.

Dress

The summer-yellow polymer dress is decorated with a green satin ribbon. The painted flowers are embellished with seed beads that match those on her purse. Beaded tassels drip from the hem.

From the Artist: Tamra Kohl

"I spent all of my childhood summers in a trailer park a couple of miles north of Ensenada, and many hours staring at every single item in the gift shop up the road. I was especially drawn to the Day of the Dead art because I thought it was funny and clever. Since then, after losing several people who were very close to me, I have come to appreciate the sentiment behind the holiday. Taking the time to joyfully celebrate and remember our deceased loved ones is such a wonderful way to keep their memories alive. In keeping with the festive attitude of the holiday, I try to capture in my own Day of the Dead sculptures the lightheartedness and humor I saw in those skeletons that I loved when I was young."

Accessories

Her stylish purse is suspended from a leather handle, lined with satin, and decorated with felt flower cutouts. Each flower is embellished with a tiny seed bead.

Bling

A strand of pearls pulls together this gal's outfit. Admire the crystal on her ring finger.

Shoes

Real leather uppers grace the shoes.

Artist: Tamra Kohl

BEYOND CLAY CALAVERAS

If clay isn't your preferred medium, you can use a wide range of other materials to create calaveras. Artists work in everything, from fragile paper to sturdy metal. Go all out and mix supplies!

Metal Drama Queen

Standing about 12" high, this metal sculpture captures a thespian emoting for all she's worth. Other of the artist's calaveras include fish, yogis, and a prisoner trying to escape a bell jar. The humor the artist brings to his metal skeletons make them seem far from cold or hard.

Artist: Brandon Kihl

Artist: Jodi Cain

Fabric and Fiber Bride and Groom

Handstitched, with vintage-button eyes, this bride and groom are dressed in outfits of fabric and leather. Their features are stitched with embroidery thread. The artist created her own pattern for the figures. You can do the same, or purchase a rag doll pattern at a fabric store. Modify it to match your vision. Sew the outfits yourself or purchase prefab doll clothing.

Sticks and Moss Couple

Sticks were used to form the arms and legs of these spectacular calaveras. Their body pieces are tied together and lightly stuffed with Spanish moss. Polymer clay heads are ornately painted. The figures' clothing is made of fabric and silk flowers, buttons, and rickrack. A trim of seed pearls embellishes them.

Artist: Denise Alvarado

FROM THE ARTIST: DENISE ALVARADO

"Día de los Muertos is a holiday rooted in the ancient past of Mesoamerica, which has rich historical imagery. My ancestors were in awe of the eternal cycle of life and death and honored those who passed on with great feasts, sacrifice, ritual, dance, and sacred art that depicted their beliefs and customs. I come by this traditional art form honestly through my earliest traceable ancestors, Aztec King Xicotencotl of Tlaxcala and Pedro de Alvarado, the Spanish conquistador. When I create Day of the Dead art, I pay homage to my ancestors and to the many indigenous people who were killed by war and lost in the process of colonization. May the flame of life smile upon the darkness of death!"

Paper Maché Catrina (Katrina)

A little paper, a little flour, and a little water were used to make this wonderful female calavera. Make your own paper maché figure by building a form out of cardboard and wire. Paper maché over the form (see the paper maché recipe on page 62). Paint and embellish.

Bread Crumb Girl

A mixture of bread crumbs and water was all that was used to create the "clay" for this simple calavera. The figure was molded and allowed to air dry before the artists painted it with acrylics.

Artists: Javier and Sandra

Artist: Carmin Gonzela

WHO IS CATRINA? (KATRINA)

Catrina calaveras are figures of elegantly dressed, wealthy women from the turn of the century. These figures satire the pretentiousness and vanity of bourgeois women of that time. They were first created by renowned Mexican artist José Guadalupe Posada. Posada's drawings mocked death, society, politics, and politicians. His images are strongly associated with Day of the Dead, and he is credited with launching the popularity of satirical calaveras.

Artist: Matt Ritchie

Artist: Matt Ritchie

Wood-Burned Spheres

This plain wooden ball was turned into a crafty piece of art with the help of wood burning tools. The artist freehand drew the design and carefully burned it into the ball. Wooden calaveras may be painted, stained, varnished, or left in their natural state.

CALAVERAS GO GREEN

The Green Movement has extended to the community of Day of the Dead artists, many of whom are using recycled items to create their calaveras. Artist Frank Pamies (Cesco) created this large calavera by taping together recycled water bottles. The figure was covered with paper maché, which also was made from recycled paper. The cracks were filled with joint compound before the piece was painted with several coats of Gesso and acrylics.

Artist: Cesco (Frank Pamies)

PAPER CALAVERA

Due to its versatility, paper is a favorite supply of many crafters. Recent interest in scrapbooking, card making, and other paper-related crafts has triggered an enormous explosion in paper products. If you want it, chances are it's available, from leathery paper to furry, glittery, or embossed patterns. Color choices are endless. Combine papers to make calaveras and to decorate a nicho home for them.

Open the closet and you just might see us hanging around, sipping Earl Grey tea.

We sit in darkness, (we really don't mind) we keep your secrets... we're deaf, dumb and blind

So please, rest assured we won't misbehave... we'll take all your dirt, with us, to the grave.

Juicy tidbits

Exhusband #1

Exhusband #2

Dirty little secrets

make me an offer

Wouldn't you like to know

Artist: Torrey Scott

Inside

Patterned paper and white paint decorate the inside of this box. A painted dowel was glued to the sides. Prefab wire hangers attach the skeletons to the rod. Cardstock pieces were inked around the edges and embellished with glitter. Skeleton shapes were cut from cardstock, painted, and assembled. Some dangle from hangers, others are adhered to the background with foam spacers to lift them slightly off of the background for added dimension.

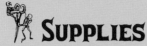

SUPPLIES

- Cigar-type box
- Art-doll die cut, or the pattern on page 136
- Dollhouse window frame
- Cloth letters
- Rub-on letters
- Small wooden clothespins
- Black, colored cardstocks and patterned paper
- Acrylic paint
- Chalk ink
- Mini brads
- Tiny metal hangers
- Adhesive

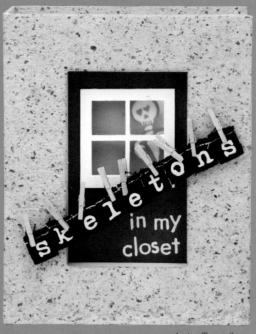

Artist: Torrey Scott

Box Container

A thrift-store chipboard box forms the basis for this nicho. The window was cut into the box, and a doll-house window frame was inserted into the hole. A piece of vellum was glued to the back side of the frame, and a skeleton figure was mounted behind. Prefab cloth letters spell out the word "skeletons." The cloth letters were sewn along a strip of ribbon and glued to the box. Tiny prefab wooden clothespins embellish. Rub-on letters form the words "in my closet."

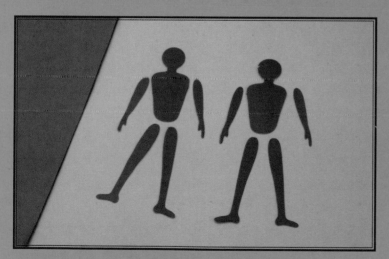

Step 1

Use a die-cut doll or the pattern on page 136 to create the skeleton shape. Trace around the figure onto black cardstock. Cut out the individual pieces. You may wish to cut the arms and legs apart at the elbow and knee joints to create even more mobile figures. Paint the skeletons as desired using chalk ink.

Step 2

Use a small hole punch to make holes in the shoulder and hip portions of the skeletons. Make similar holes in the tops of the arms and leg sections. Insert mini brads through the holes and bend back the tabs to secure.

DECORATIVE NICHOS

Some calaveras are free-natured souls who stand happily in any environment. Others are homebodies who are best displayed in a well-designed setting. A nicho is a home for your calavera. Most often the nicho is a simple box constructed of either metal or wood. It can be elaborately painted, or decorated more simplistically. Look for ways to utilize a variety of textures and colors in your decorating scheme.

A Perfect Puzzle

Bare puzzle pieces, available in many hobby stores, were stamped with the Spanish words for lust, gluttony, sloth, wrath, envy, and pride, before being adhered to the back of this nicho. Typewriter letters glued to the top of the box spell out the Spanish word for death. The scene is adorned with clock hands.

TRY THIS

Can't find the right size container for your nicho? Make your own! The nichos on these pages were constructed with simple baseboard moldings, available at hardware and lumber stores. If you aren't handy with a saw, use foam core, cardboard, or chipboard instead of wood.

Artist: Michelle Ritchie

Clay, Clay, and More Clay

A polymer clay calavera of Frida Kahlo, one of Mexico's most beloved artists, is housed in a rustic nicho decorated with a clay skeleton cactus, and wings.

Artist: Michelle Ritchie

Artist: Michelle Ritchie

Artist: Michelle Ritchie

Theme-Related Found Items

The king and queen of hearts cards decorate this darling nicho while paying honor to the bride and groom. The red background was stamped with tiny skulls.

Plush Felt Heart

Fabric was used to create the heart backdrop for this calavera love scene. Glittery dots outline the edges of the heart.

COLLAGE A NICHO

This plain box is painted black, splattered with green acrylic paint, lined with hot pink satin, and then decorated with wonderful collaged images. You can use a shoe or gift box, or create your own box by cutting and gluing together pieces of foam core. Many craft stores also sell plain, inexpensive wooden boxes.

Title, Figures, and Flowers

The title of this nicho was created with glitter, bottle caps, and wooden circles embellished with rhinestone letters that spell out the word *amigas*, Spanish for friends. Clip art, magazine clippings, stickers, and drawings were combined to create the collaged calaveras, family car trip scene, juke box, dog, and saddle shoe collages. Decoupaged elements were carefully cut out, matted, layered, and embellished before being glued to a piece of black cardstock that was mounted on the nicho. Learn more about decoupaging elements, such as the flower decorations, on the opposite page.

 SUPPLIES

- Wooden box
- Black acrylic paint and green acrylic paint for the box
- Satin to line the inside of the wooden box
- Chipboard or wooden façade cut to fit around the face of the wooden box
- Clip art, magazine clippings, and stickers
- Black and colored cardstocks
- Paper, pens, and paint for decorating collaged elements
- Colored jewels

Artist: Pamela Hauer

Step 1

To create the petals, freehand cut five ¾" circles from magazine pictures and printed papers. Cut three additional slightly smaller circles.

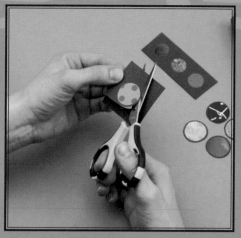

Step 2

Adhere all eight petals to black cardstock and then freehand cut around them, leaving a small black border.

Step 3

Adhere the five larger petals together, overlapping them in a flower pattern.

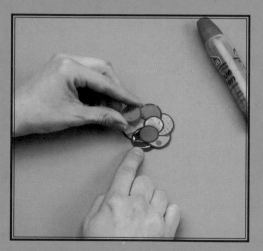

Step 4

Adhere the three smaller petals to the larger petal platform, overlapping the small petals into a flower shape.

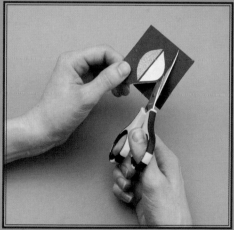

Step 5

Make a leaf by cutting two halves out of magazine pictures or printed papers and adhering them together onto black cardstock. Trim around them, as in Step 2. Adhere the leaf to the back of the flower.

Step 6

Cut a tiny circle from black cardstock and adhere it to the center of the flower. Finish by gluing a rhinestone to the black center.

Artist: Pam Hauer

Masks and Skulls

Decorative Pieces to Display or Wear

If it's difficult for you to imagine decorating your home with skulls, take a closer look at the wonderful skull masks and full head skulls that are an important part of Day of the Dead celebrations! These pieces are beautifully crafted and often highly embellished. Day of the Dead skull folk art is usually far less realistic than skeleton masks worn by eager trick-or-treaters on Halloween. Traditionally, they are wildly painted in festive colors.

Because Day of the Dead masks and skulls are so ornate and unusual, they make wonderful additions to household décor year-round. Hang your masks as a collection for dramatic impact, spread them through-out your home, or create an ofrenda-like display that includes both masks and skulls.

Open Your Mind to the Possibilities

The good, the bad, and the ugly…Day of the Dead masks and skulls are that and more! They may be made of plaster, paper maché, paper, or even gourds. While many are brightly painted, some artists choose to break tradition with pieces that are black-and-white or earth tone. You needn't be an accomplished mask maker to create a Day of the Dead mask or skull. Prefabricated masks, available in most hobby stores, make it easy to form the basic shape of your piece. Modify the shape and decorate it to make it your own.

Colorful Plaster Mask

"I love the beauty of all Day of the Dead art. It's romantic and beautiful and celebrates death instead of mourning it," says artist Missy Robinson. Her plaster skull/mask was formed using a sugar skull mold. It was then painted hot pink and varnished to a glossy sheen.

Artist: Missy Robinson

Artist: Pam Hauer

Store Bought Skull

"I must have been about 14, and initially the bright and fun colors and themes of the Day of the Dead art were what I was drawn to—besides the fact that I have always been partial to skulls. Don't know why, maybe a therapist could explain it!" says artist Pam Hauer. She purchased this plastic model skull and then painted it with acrylics to give it a festive air.

Endearingly Impressionistic Mask

"San Francisco has a great Day of the Dead parade each year, and I wanted to have a mask of my own to wear to it," says Jenn Rodriguez. She created this mask out of paper maché. The oversized eyes add to the mask's approachable "ET-like" quality.

Artist: Jenn Rodriguez

Softball Size Personalities

Rows of paper maché skulls line tables at artisans' booths in Los Angeles at dozens of Day of the Dead celebrations. While the skull shapes are very simplistic, the intricate painting jobs give each a distinct personality.

Artist: Unknown, 6th Street Festival

ALL SAINTS' DAY, ALL SOULS' DAY, DAY OF THE DEAD, AND HALLOWEEN

Because all four of these holidays are celebrated in late October and early November, and appear to share some of the same traditions, it is easy to confuse one with another.

All Saints' Day: Established by Pope Boniface IV in 609/610 to honor all the saints, known and unknown. It is observed on November 1 with song and prayer.

All Souls' Day: Established in 1048 by St. Odilo of Cluny as a day to pray for souls who are caught in purgatory. It is celebrated November 2.

Day of the Dead: Originated approximately 3000 years ago with the Aztecs and then evolved with the intervention of the Catholic Church. The holiday joyfully welcomes back the souls of loved ones with prayer, food, dance, and the decorating of graves.

Halloween: Originally called All-Hallow-Even, it was a pagan holiday that marked a time to take stock of supplies and slaughter livestock for winter. It was believed by some that on this day the boundaries between the world of the living and dead overlapped and the deceased could return to do evil deeds. It is celebrated October 31, most popularly with trick-or-treating and pumpkin carving.

Paper Maché Mask

Paper machéing is a no-fail way to create a variety of crafts, including masks and skulls. Paper maché is so simple to use that most of us were first introduced to it in elementary school. While there are commercial paper maché mixes available, it is easiest and least expensive to make your own by mixing flour, water, and salt together to form a thick glue. To make your own paper maché mask, follow the instructions on the opposite page. Turning your mask into a full skull requires a few extra steps. You'll find those on page 64.

 Supplies

- Paper maché paste (One cup flour, two cups water, two T. salt. Mix together until it forms a thick glue, the consistency of pudding. Add more flour if paste is runny. Continue to stir until all lumps are removed.)
- Torn strips of newspaper
- Skull or mask form
- 1-2 round balloons
- Tape
- Napkins
- Gesso (acrylic primer)
- Acrylic paints
- Paintbrushes
- Spray varnish
- Craft knife

Artist: Jerry Vigil

Step 1

Blow up a balloon to approximate the size of the back part of a skull. Fit the balloon to a prefabricated mask, positioning the balloon's opening under the chin area of the mask. Tape the balloon to the mask.

Step 2

Dip strips of newspaper in paper maché paste. Slide the strips of paper between two fingers to remove extra paste. Lay strips of the newspaper along the seam between the mask and the balloon. When finished, lay strips over the rest of the mask, covering the eye sockets and mouth, but leaving the nose exposed.

Step 3

Soak napkins in paper maché paste. Squeeze and form them into appropriate shapes. Lay them across the mask to make cheekbones, eye orbs, lips, and teeth.

Step 4

Lay more newspaper strips dipped in paste over the napkin shapes. Smooth as you go. Allow to dry. Pop the balloon and remove the prefab mask from the form. Paint.

If you plan to turn your mask into a full skull, turn the page for further instructions.

Turn Your Paper Maché Mask Into a Skull

Unlike a mask, a skull can be displayed on a table or bookcase. Turn the mask that you've created into a skull with only a few additional steps. After popping the original balloon and removing it and the prefab mask from your mask shape, blow up a second balloon. Tape it, as you did before, so that it forms the back section of the skull. Follow the directions below, to make the rest of the skull.

Step 1

Roll or wad dry newspaper and tape it to form a circle. Tape the circular piece to the base of the skull.

Step 2

Cover the newspaper circle and tape with several lays of paper maché strips. Allow to dry. Pop the balloon.

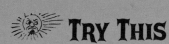 TRY THIS

Use a firm brush when applying the base coats of white to your mask or skull. Once the paint wets down the paper maché, you will be able to press out many ripples and other flaws.

Step 3

Apply up to three coats of thick white paint or Gesso. Allow to dry. Paint features on the mask or skull with acrylic paint. Finish by spraying on a sealer such as varnish.

Another Sassy Skelly Mask

An upbeat paint job and a couple of paper flowers turn this potentially scary mask into one that inspires smiles. The mask's broad face was created by laying paper maché over a handmade dome-shaped paper clay base. The features were added to the paper maché layer in the same manner as the mask on page 63. Once dried, the paper maché mask was lifted from the paper clay base. The paper clay base could then be reused.

Artist: Jerry Vigil

Think BIG

BIG may or may not be better, but it sure can be fun when playing with paper maché! Once you feel comfortable working with it, try making something life-sized or even larger. Taking up residence in the corner of your home, a super-sized paper maché Day of the Dead figure, like this, makes it clear that you're not at all shy about displaying your cool artwork.

Artist: Unknown, Festival de la Gente

PAINT YOUR MASK OR SKULL

It's difficult to look at a newly dried paper maché creation and imagine how compelling it will be when completed. But all it takes to turn a pulpy-looking mask or skull shape into a true piece of folk art are a few coats of paint to cover the newsprint and a few more to add color and character. Most artists favor acrylic paint for decorating their work because it is easy to apply and cleans up with soap and water. There are hundreds of colors of acrylics at your local hobby store. Invest in a few good brushes of different sizes. Have fun. Remember, you can always re-prime the artwork and begin again if your first attempts don't meet your standards.

Artist: Andrea Zocchi

SUPPLIES

- Paper maché mask, see page 62
- Pencil
- Gesso (acrylic primer)
- Fine, medium, and large acrylic paintbrushes
- Acrylic paints
- Plastic palette
- Spray varnish

Step 1

Use a large brush to prime your mask, creating a smooth, clean work surface for your design.

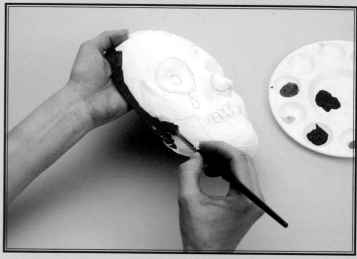

Step 2

Lightly pencil in the design you will be painting.

Step 3

Begin by painting in the larger areas of your design. Allow those areas to dry before moving on to more detailed work. Dry thoroughly.

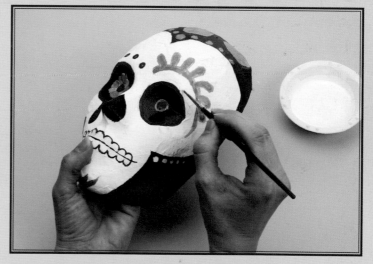

Step 4

Use water to dilute brown paint. Gently brush the diluted paint over the lighter colors on your mask in order to give those areas depth.

Step 5

Touch up any white portions of the mask that appear smudged. Make sure all pencil lines have been covered with paint. Protect the mask with a coat of spray varnish.

Decorate Your Mask or Skull

There are endless ways to decorate your mask or skull. Most involve at least a bit of painting. Artists also use elements such as charms, glitter letters, brads, and patterned and specialty papers favored by scrapbookers and paper artists. But it isn't necessary to purchase all of the embellishments. Chances are your home is filled with things that, with a creative eye, you can add to your artwork. Check out your junk drawers for screws, nails, washers, bag ties, old pencils, or gum wrappers. Your jewelry box undoubtedly holds broken earrings and necklaces you no longer wear. Bathroom drawers, with hair ties, barrettes, and clips, offer up oodles of treasures. Keep your eyes open at thrift stores and garage sales for additional pieces to add to your embellishment hoard.

Embellish With Fabric and Ribbon

A broken brooch was mounted to the forehead of this mask over a felt petal-shaped foundation. The centers of other fabric flowers were adorned with glitter dots.

Base Before embellishing, this mask was painted a creamy white. The eye sockets were painted black.

Eyes, Flowers, and Leaves Reproduction oilcloth was used to create the two-dimensional flowers and leaves on the mask. Each element was cut from the cloth and glued down separately. Vintage plastic jewelry flowers were glued to the centers of the eye sockets.

Mouth Three different types of ribbon were layered and glued to the mask to form the mouth.

Artist: Pam Hauer

Artist: Pam Hauer

Embellish With Metal

Pieces of old jewelry were added to this mask for dimension and gleam. Some pieces were disassembled and smaller sections were used separately. A cloth flower adorned with a clip-on earring was added to the upper portion of the mask.

Base Gold acrylic craft paint was used to paint all but the eyes of the mask. The eyes were painted black. Silver and black permanent markers were used to add swirling patterns and dots.

Eyes Pieces of vintage jewelry were layered and glued together to create eyes before they were adhered to the mask.

Mouth A cast-off metal choker necklace was stretched across the mask and adhered to create the illusion of teeth.

Embellish With Found Elements

Dice beads, charms, rhinestones, and other found elements decorate this mask, along with purple stars cut from glittered paper. The guitar pick goatee and horns (plastic teeth) were the finishing touches.

Base A coat of black paint was used to cover this mask before flame shapes were added with acrylic craft paint. Translucent purple glitter paint was added over remaining black areas.

Eyes The eyes were created with poker chips. A circle of leopard print paper was layered on top. Skull stickers were adhered to the center of the printed paper, and the skeleton's eyes were embellished with rhinestones.

Mouth The mouth was created by cutting and gluing a piece of prismatic paper to the mask. A black piece of cardstock was trimmed to follow the irregular lines of the prismatic paper and then glued in place. Individual white cardstock "teeth" were cut and glued to the cardstock. The mouth was detailed with a black pen.

Artist: Pam Hauer

FROM THE ARTIST: PAM HAUER

"As a teenager, a Mexican Folk Art shop opened up within walking distance of my house. I spent many an afternoon in there perusing all the beautiful art and handcrafts, especially the Day of the Dead stuff. Also, as a teen, my Dad took me to Pirate Gallery (Denver) a lot, including their Annual Day of the Dead fest. So, as I learned more about the actual reason for the holiday, I thought that part of it was really cool too—it was a thoughtful and helpful way to help the living deal with the loss of loved ones and to honor and remember them creatively."

Artist: Pam Hauer

Embellish With Beads

Tiny flowers and beads were strung together before being glued around the edges of this mask. A vintage brooch was glued to the forehead. Additional beads, a tiara, and earrings were added.

Base This mask was painted black before beadwork was added. After all beaded elements were in place, the remaining areas were painted with adhesive and covered with pink micro beads.

Eyes Small mirrors surrounded by embroidered borders form the center of the eyes. A narrow band of glitter frames them. The eyes were then outlined with sequins, seed beads, and rhinestones, glued on individually. Seed beads were glued to the remaining portion of the eyes.

Mouth The lips were lined with blue seed beads, glued on individually. Red bugle beads were adhered inside the lip outline. The lips were then coated with a dimensional glaze.

Wood Burn a Gourd Mask

Gourds have been used by humans throughout history as musical instruments, vessels, birdhouses, and decorative objects. When dried and cleaned, they can also be turned into beautiful Day of the Dead masks. Gourd masks can be painted, carved, or decorated with beads, feathers, and other colorful embellishments. They can also be decorated using an inexpensive wood-burning tool. The shape of the gourd helps determine the shapes of the features you'll work into the mask. You can create your patterns by freehand drawing on the gourd, or with stamps and stencils. Combine these options for greater creative flexibility.

 Supplies

- Gourd
- Hand saw
- Dust mask
- Safety glasses
- Metal spoon
- Pencil
- Electric rotary tool or keyhole saw
- Wood-burning tool
- Stamps, stencils
- Pigment stamping ink
- Leather dye
- Buffing towel

 Try This

If you are lucky enough to have a large backyard garden, you can plant your own gourds. Leave them on their vines to dry and then remove them to a well-ventilated shelf to finish the process. Wear a mask to clean a dried gourd. Wash it with plain soap and water, or add some bleach. Scrape the surface with stiff brushes or the back of a kitchen knife.

Artist: Kerry Arquette

Step 1

Use a hand saw to cut a gourd in half. Dried gourds have a high mold content; be sure to wear a dust mask. Scrape the inside of the gourd clean with a metal spoon.

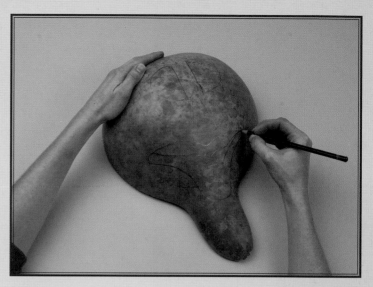

Step 2

Freehand draw a face onto the gourd just as you would a pumpkin.

Step 3

Remove the eyes and other features using an electric rotary tool or keyhole saw. Be sure to use the proper safety equipment, such as safety glasses and a dust mask. If the gourd is thin enough, you may try to cut the openings with a utility knife.

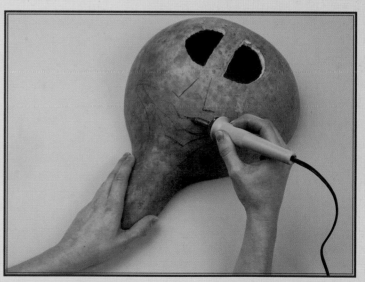

Step 4

Use a wood-burning tool to trace the mouth and nose.

Step 5

Decorate by stamping. To re-create this look, work on images individually. Stamp the image. Allow it to dry for a minute and then trace the design with the wood-burning tool.

Step 6

Stencils may also be used to create designs. Hold the stencil in place, or tape it to the gourd. Trace around the stencil with a pencil and then re-trace with the wood-burning tool.

Step 7

Fill in blank areas with doodles created with the wood-burning tool. Add color with leather dye applied with cotton swabs. Allow to dry. Be careful not to stain your hands with dye.

Step 8

Buff with a towel to create a sheen.

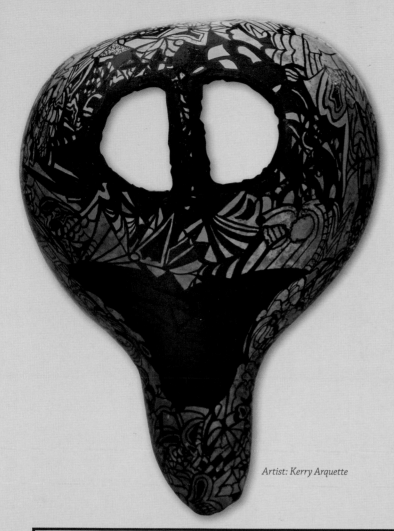

Painting a Gourd Mask

If decoratively burning a gourd isn't your style, you can still create a wonderful Day of the Dead gourd mask with indelible markers and acrylic paints. Use the marker to freehand draw features. Continue with the marker, creating patterns until you are satisfied. Fill in selected areas with acrylic paints, or go wild and paint the entire mask!

Artist: Kerry Arquette

WHERE TO BUY GOURDS

Growing gourds takes space and time. If you are short on either of those commodities, it is best to purchase your gourd. An online search for "buy/purchase craft gourds" provides a list of sellers, and online auction sites list gourds for sale. The Internet will also lead you to any gourd farms in your area. A trip to the farm is a wonderful outing. Gourds are priced based on size, symmetry, and general appearance.

Photo-Collaged Mask

Scrapbooking and other types of memory art utilize photos to celebrate and commemorate the important people in our lives. Day of the Dead also focuses on remembering the lives of those who touch our own. A Day of the Dead mask collaged with a collection of images spanning the lifetime of a family member or friend honors the person in a unique way. Begin your photo-collaged mask by creating a basic paper maché foundation. Cover the dried mask form with black-and-white photocopies of old images. The more diverse the photos, the more interesting your mask will be.

 Supplies

- Paper maché paste (see recipe for paper maché paste on page 62)
- Halloween skull decoration or mask
- Paper towels
- Torn strips of newspaper
- Gesso (acrylic primer)
- Black-and-white copies of photos
- Decoupage medium
- Paintbrush
- Craft knife
- Glitter paint or pigments
- Acrylic paints or acrylic paint pens
- Jewels and other embellishments
- Spray varnish

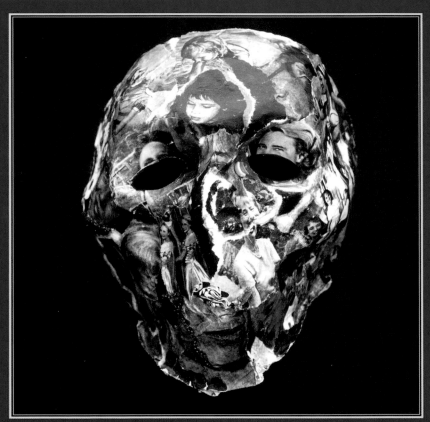

Artist: Kerry Arquette

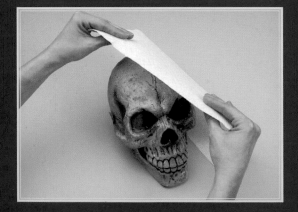

Step 1

Lay pieces of paper towel over a decorative Halloween skull or mask. This is necessary when building upon a prefab mask that isn't slick and smooth. Without the covering towel the paper maché will stick to the foundation.

Step 2

Coat strips of newspaper in paper maché paste. Lay the strips across the front portion of the skull, leaving the back part of the skull free of paper maché. Continue until you have achieved your desired thickness. Allow to dry. Remove the mask from the skull. Paint the mask white with Gesso.

Step 3

Rip around the edges of your photocopied photos. You may wish to rip a single photo into several pieces for effect. Collage ripped pieces to the skull using decoupage medium. Leave ragged seams between some photos, allowing the white paper maché skull to show through. Allow to dry.

Step 4

Cut eye openings with a craft knife. Mix shimmery pigment paints with a bit of decoupage medium. Paint selected portions of seams.

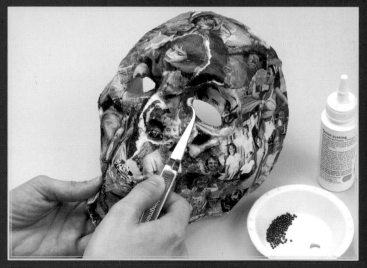

Step 5

Glue small jewels at the corner of one eye. Glue additional jewels along a few select seams. Spray your completed mask with a sealant to protect it from humidity and dirt.

TASTY SUGAR SKULLS

Sugar skulls are a traditional part of Day of the Dead celebrations. During the week before the holiday, piles of colorfully decorated skulls in a variety of sizes are sold for nibbling and also to decorate ofrendas. Skulls come in a range of sizes and styles. They may be complete heads, tiny masks, or even full skeletons reclining in glittery sugar coffins. Some sugar skulls intended for display rather than consumption are decorated with colored foil, feathers or sequins.

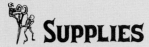

SUPPLIES

- Mixing bowl
- Measuring spoons and cups
- Water
- White granulated sugar
- Meringue powder
- Sugar skull molds (available online in several sizes)
- Cardboard
- Gel food coloring
- Powdered sugar
- Icing bag and applicator tip
- Embellishments

Artist: Unknown, Olvera Street

Step 1

Inside a bowl, mix 1 teaspoon meringue powder and 1 cup of sugar. Dampen with enough water to create an even consistency similar to sand. (Meringue powder is sold in many hobby stores and is also available online. It is absolutely necessary in the creation of sugar skulls, and substitutions will not work.)

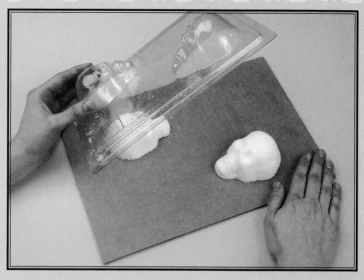

Step 2

Press the mixture into the molds and scrape off the excess.

Step 3

Cover the exposed mold with a piece of cardboard and carefully invert. Lift the mold away from the sugar skulls and allow them to dry overnight.

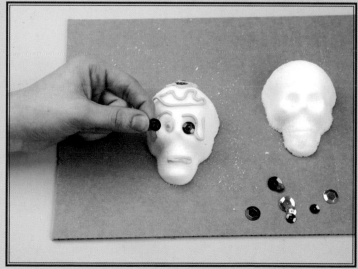

Step 4

Mix powdered sugar with food coloring. Decorate as desired.

Step 5

If your sugar skull will not be eaten, continue to decorate with jewels, beads, feathers, foil, and other accessories.

Artist: Kerry Arquette

JEWELRY

Necklaces, Earrings & Bracelets

Day of the Dead jewelry is guaranteed to be a conversation starter. Most pieces include traditional Day of the Dead symbols such as skulls, marigolds, crosses, and images of saints. They bring the holiday to mind each time you wear them. Jewelry may be created with clay, beads, or metal. However, inspired crafters have begun working with unusual materials, including fabric and tape. Because of the wide range of designs and materials used in making the pieces, they can be worn with casual outfits and also with more formal attire.

Whether you are drawn to dainty or more dramatic and substantial pieces, there are many styles of Day of the Dead jewelry projects from which to choose. Most of the ideas in this chapter are made with tools and supplies you may already have around the house. Others are readily available at your local craft or hardware store. Consider buying enough supplies for more than one version of each project. Friends and family members will be putting in orders for your custom creations.

From Sophisticated to Silly

Day of the Dead jewelry may be punk. It may be upscale, but it is never stodgy. Like all crafts associated with the holiday, it doesn't take itself too seriously. Even behind a finely crafted sterling silver charm, there lurks a good-natured wink. Making Day of the Dead jewelry calls for more creativity than cash, so be ready to invest your wry sense of humor in each piece you create. You'll find yourself taking risks and expanding on ideas as you become more and more comfortable with the process of making your own jewelry.

Pretty Pendant

"This 1920s-looking photo inspired me to create something thrift-store chic for Day of the Dead," says artist Kerry Arquette. One band bracket was snipped off this secondhand wristwatch. The watch was disassembled so that a photo could be tucked inside. The skull image on the outside of the watch crystal was created with a photo-transfer technique. The image was printed on an inkjet printer. (If you have a laser-jet printer, photocopy the image.) Clear packing tape was adhered to the top of the skull image and burnished with the back of a spoon. It was then placed in a bowl of warm water for several minutes. Once the paper softened, it was gently rubbed free of the tape. The skull image remained on the tape. When dry, the tape was trimmed to size and adhered to the crystal with decoupage medium. The watch was reassembled and embellished with ribbon and charms.

Artist: Kerry Arquette

Bottle Cap Whimsy

"I love making my bottle-cap characters and relate to them the same way I did to my paper dolls as a child," says artist Ramona Hotel. The Day of the Dead skeleton's head was created by squeezing a bottle cap around a laminated skull picture. The body was formed with hammered bottle caps, and the legs and arms, from copper tubing. All the pieces were connected with copper wire.

Artist: Ramona Hotel

Artist: Kerry Arquette

Cool Cuff

"I have the kind of daughters who would never wear anything shiny and girly," says artist Kerry Arquette. "This Day of the Dead cuff is just up their style alley." The cuff was created by overlaying a strip of prism vinyl with clip-art images. Clear packing tape was stretched across the top of the images. Black electrical tape overlaps the edges. Felt, glued to the inside of the cuff, prevents chaffing. Velcro® was glued in place for the closure.

Demure Bracelets

"I love the results when delicate candy-colored beads are combined with a Day of the Dead theme," says artist Jamie Marsh. Although these bracelets look complicated, they were actually made by repeating a simple beading pattern over and over again until the bracelet reaches the desired length. The tiny skull beads dangling from the bracelets are just one of many styles available in most bead stores.

Artist: Jamie Marsh

HERITAGE MEMORY NECKLACE

Combine colorful beads with a heritage photo for an arresting piece of jewelry that is both thoughtful and playful. Before making the heritage pendant, create the necklace by stringing beads along a length of jewelry wire. Attach jewelry clasps to each end. Follow the directions on the right to make the dangling memory charm.

 ## SUPPLIES

- Felt beads
- Tweezers
- Scissors
- Jewelry wire
- Wire cutter
- Jewelry pliers
- Jewelry clasp
- Variety of plastic and metal beads
- Skull beads
- Heritage photo
- Wooden spool
- Decoupage medium
- Silver bead and charm
- Jump rings

Artist: Erikia Ghumm

FROM THE ARTIST: ERIKIA GHUMM

"I absolutely love Day of the Dead because it encompasses so many things I adore. For me, it's all about remembering family members and celebrating their lives, the art, the symbolism, and the spirit of the holiday. These aspects are the basis for a lot of art I create, be it a scrapbook page, a piece of jewelry, or a mixed-media assemblage."

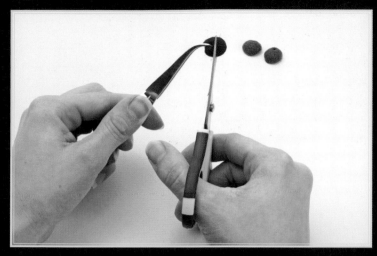

Step 1

Use tweezers to hold a felt bead while cutting it in half with scissors.

Step 2

Reduce and trim a heritage photo to fit around a wooden spool. Adhere the photo to the spool with decoupage medium.

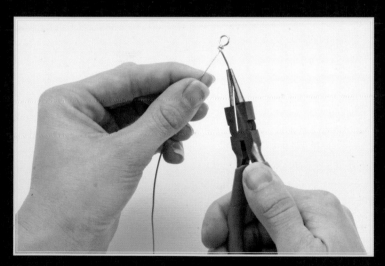

Step 3

Cut a piece of wire the length of your spool, plus 4-5". Use pliers to pinch the wire 1" from one end. Wrap the short end of the wire around the pliers to form a loop. Continue to wrap the short end of the wire along the longer one until there is no more wire with which to work.

Step 4

Thread one half of the cut felt bead onto the wire until it stops at the loop you just created. Follow with the spool. Add another of the cut felt beads and a smaller decorative silver bead. Create another wire-wrapped loop. Use a short piece of wire or a jump ring to attach your silver charm to the bottom of the beaded spool and another to connect the spool to the beaded necklace.

Microscope Slide Earrings

Every time you turn your head, these little skeletons will dance. Their swing is downright jaunty, and that suits the atmosphere surrounding the Day of the Dead perfectly. Use images in the back of this book, purchase and download clip art, or draw your own. These images were printed onto transparencies, but could also be printed on shrink plastic or fabric.

Supplies

- Day of the Dead images
- Transparency sheet
- Scissors
- 2 glass microscope slides
- Chipboard
- Paint, ink, etc. (optional)
- Silver tape
- Flux
- Soldering iron
- Jump ring
- Beads
- Earring hook
- Jewelry pliers
- Buffing wax

Try This

When printing on transparencies, be sure to use the appropriate type of transparency for your printer. Transparencies are available for both inkjet and laserjet printers; printing on the wrong transparency could destroy your printer.

Artist: Laura McKinley

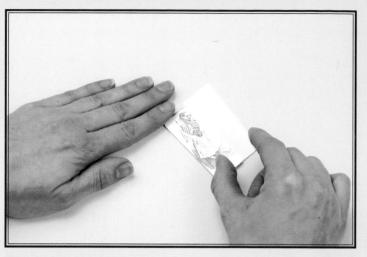

Step 1

Size your image to fit behind the microscope slide and print it onto a transparency. Silhouette cut the focal character.

Step 2

Trim a piece of chipboard to match the size of the microscope slide. Decorate the back of the chipboard as desired or leave it blank. Sandwich the skeleton image between the microscope slide and the chipboard.

Step 3

Wrap the perimeter of the microscope slide and chipboard with silver tape and paint it with liquid flux. Solder the edge. Solder on a jump ring.

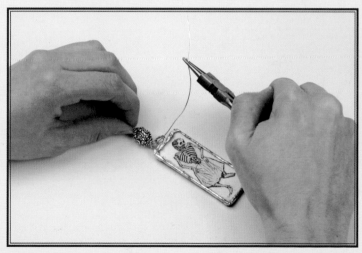

Step 4

Embellish with a silver bead and an earring hook, using a jump ring and wire-wrapping to attach it. Finish with buffing wax.

Marigold Beaded Necklace

Three types of handmade polymer clay beads were strung together to create this stunning necklace. The stark white skull is the focal point of the piece, with the orange marigold and black-and-white checkered beads creating contrast through both color and pattern. Creating the beads takes a bit of time, but they require no painting after they are baked.

Supplies

- Clay sculpting tools
- Polymer clay
  Ivory (2 ounces)
  Lightest color (1 ounce)
  Light color (2 ounces)
  Dark color (4 ounces)
  Waste (4 ounces)
  White (2-4 ounces)
  Black (2-4 ounces)
- Jewelry wire
- Jewelry clasp
- Jewelry pliers

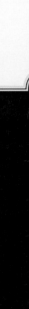

Artist: Kari Hansen

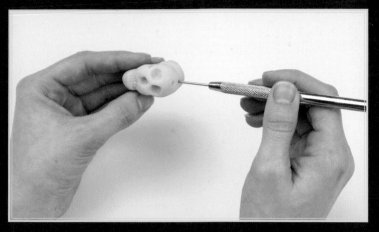

Step 1

Skull Bead: Create the skull with ivory polymer clay, as shown on page 35. Once sculpted, poke a hole through the vertical center of the skull. Bake according to manufacturer's directions.

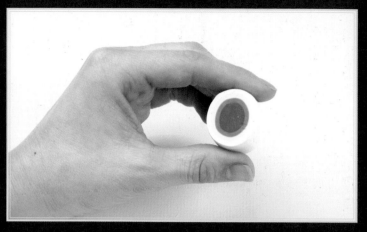

Step 2

Marigold Petals: Make the petals with all four colors of polymer clay (approx. 1 ounce of ivory, lightest and light color, and 2 ounces of dark color). Roll out thin sheets of each color. Layer the rolled clay sheets on top of each other beginning with the ivory. Follow with the lightest shade and move to the darkest. Pinch the layers into a tube shape.

Step 3

Reduce the size of the tube by squeezing and pulling on the clay in a milking fashion to make it narrower and longer. Cut it into six equal pieces.

Step 4

Marigold Center: Create the marigold center in a similar manner as the marigold petal, however using only the two darkest colors of clay (approx. 1 ounce light and 1 ounce dark). Reduce the tube and cut it to match the length of the marigold petal pieces. To create the exterior stripped wrap, roll out light yellow clay. Layer narrow strips of dark orange and light yellow on top of the rolled out clay. Smooth together. Wrap the exterior piece around the outside of the marigold center.

Step 5

Place the six marigold petals (step 3) around a marigold center (step 4).

Step 6

Cover with a thin layer of dark clay (approx. 1 ounce) and smooth to remove all of the ridges and depressions. Add thin snakes of dark orange to fill in each depression. Add another thin sheet of dark orange to cover the entire assemblage. Reduce to desired size and thinly slice.

Step 7

Use waste clay to roll a round ball (approx. 2 ounces). Place slices of the marigold around the outside of the ball (left) and roll to smooth the pieces together (right). Poke a hole through the center. Bake according to manufacturer's directions.

Step 8

Checkered Beads: Use white and black clay (approx. 2-4 ounces of each). Create six snakes of each color. Lay three of the snakes down side by side, alternating colors. Add 3 more layers of alternating snakes on top. Gently squeeze the layers together.

Step 9

Reduce the joined pieces to the desired size, as in step 3. Thinly slice the checkered tube.

Step 10

Use waste clay to roll a ball (approx. 2 ounces). Place slices of the checkered tube around the outside of the ball and roll to smooth the pieces together. Poke a hole through the center. Bake according to manufacturer's directions. String all of the beads onto jewelry wire and add a clasp.

From the Artist: Kari Hansen

"Day of the Dead artwork is a joy to create because of its fusion of tradition and individuality. New to Day of the Dead festivities, I found working on its artwork both challenging and stimulating, since it inspired me to work with motifs and color combinations I may not normally explore. Like the celebration itself, the artwork longs to be dramatic, vibrant, and full of personal expression. Its lively colors, dynamic symbolism, and festive themes provide an opportunity to let creativity run wild. There is a freedom in knowing that you really can't go too 'over the top' in Day of the Dead pieces!"

Three Original Charms

Are they called "charms" because they hold some special power or because they are utterly charming? Either way, they are certainly a favorite piece of jewelry for people of all cultures. Whether worn solo at the end of a necklace or combined with an array of others for a bracelet, Day of the Dead charms are tiny pieces of eye candy.

 **Supplies**

Wooden Cross Charm
- Wooden cross charm
- 1 ounce polymer clay
- Acrylic paints
- Paintbrush
- Black permanent marker

Virgin in a Bottle Charm
- Small image of the Virgin of Guadalupe
- Small apothecary jar or vial with stopper
- Silk flower petals
- Copper wire
- Wire cutters
- Jewelry tweezers
- Beads
- Jump rings

Beaded Skeleton Charm
- Headpin
- Skull bead
- Sturdy silver wire
- Turquoise bead
- Colorful beads (approximately 24)
- Jewelry tweezers
- Jump rings

Artist: Karen Hickerson

Step 1

Wooden Cross Charm: Condition polymer clay until it is warm and pliable. Roll two small circles of clay—one for a small skull and one to form the base of the charm.

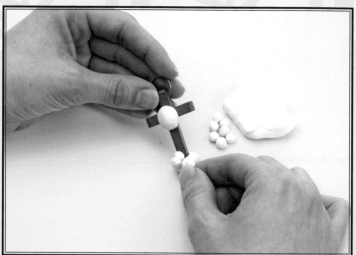

Step 2

Press the wooden cross charm into the clay base. Make the skull (as seen on page 35) and press onto the front of the cross charm. To create the marigolds, roll several small circles of clay and press them around the base of the charm and directly on the cross. Bake according to manufacturer's directions.

Step 3

Using a fine-tipped paintbrush, begin painting the marigolds with green, yellow, and red.

Step 4

Finish detailing the charm by adding facial features to the skull with a fine-tipped permanent marker.

Step 1

Virgin in a Bottle Charm: Download an image of the Virgin de Guadalupe and reduce it to fit on a small apothecary jar. Print the image and glue it to the jar. Trim the petals from a yellow silk flower and insert them into the jar.

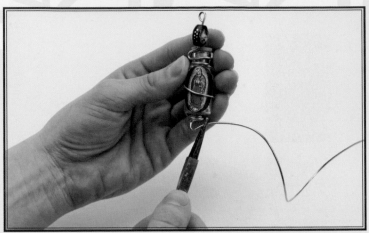

Step 2

Use jewelry tweezers to create a loop at the end of a piece of copper wire. Slide a bead onto the wire, positioning it below the loop. Wrap the length of copper wire around the jar in a spiral design. Tighten the spiral at the base of the charm. Create another wire loop. Cut away extra wire.

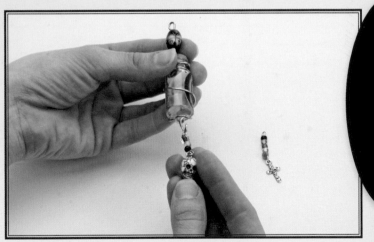

Step 3

Create dangling charms by making a loop at one end of a short piece of wire. Attach a charm to the loop with a jump ring. Thread beads onto the wire. Make a loop to prevent the beads from falling off. Use a jump ring to attach that loop to the loop at the bottom of the jar.

Step 1

Beaded Skeleton Charm: To make a tri-loop bar, use your tweezers to create loops in the ends of a short piece of sturdy wire. Create the center loop by crossing the ends of the wire, as though you were beginning to tie your shoe. Pull gently until the center loop is the right size. Thread a skull bead onto a silver headpin. Thread the headpin through the center loop of your bar and add a turquoise bead.

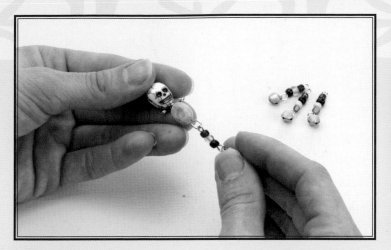

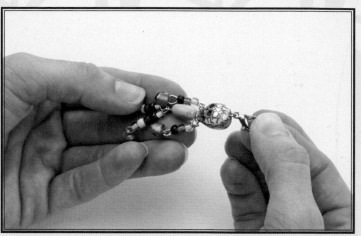

Step 2

Make a loop with the headpin wire extending below the bead. Cut off excess wire. To make arms and legs, create a loop in a short piece of wire. Thread small beads onto the wire and make a loop at the other end. Use a jump ring to attach a bell to one loop, and use a jump ring attach the piece to the body. Repeat to make the other limbs.

Step 3

Attach a jump ring to the top of the charm.

THE HISTORY OF CHARMS

Roman Empire Christians use fish charms to gain entry into secluded religious services. Jewish scholars carry passages of Jewish law inside amulets worn around their necks.

Middle Ages Knights and kings believe in the dark powers of charms, using them to cast spells on enemy territories or to protect knights in battle.

Renaissance While unfavored by the more educated upper classes, the lower classes still believe in the superstitions and supposed magical powers of charms.

Industrial Revolution Charms are manufactured for the wealthy as popular status symbols.

Mid-1800s Charms become very fashionable as Queen Victoria popularizes the look of lockets, family crests, and jewels.

WWII Soldiers bring back little trinkets for their sweeties, setting off a charm-making surge among U.S. jewelers.

1940s Toy charms start falling out of gumball machines, and children begin wearing them on bracelets and necklaces.

1950s Teenage girls are gifted a charm bracelet to mark milestones, such as Sweet 16s, graduations, and weddings. These are called "lifetime" bracelets, and charms are added to signify each milestone.

1990s Vintage charms are the rage as people begin snapping them up from antique and thrift stores and, of course, eBay.

FABRIC JEWELRY

Day of the Dead-themed fabric, with its bright colors and preprinted patterns, makes creating jewelry easy. Use entire motifs within a design or cut out portions of the pattern. Use the Day of the Dead fabric to cover beads and clay pendants. Look online for the widest selection and best prices. Since jewelry requires only small pieces of fabric, purchase remnants to save money.

Fabric Skull Pendant

"Pendants are the perfect way to use fabric with larger patterns," says artist Kerry Arquette. This polymer clay pendant was formed, pierced, and baked before being covered with a skull image from Day of the Dead fabric. The image was cut from a swath of Day of the Dead fabric (below) and attached to the clay pendant with decoupage medium. It was then embellished with beads and hung from a cord created by braiding strips of Day of the Dead-themed fabric.

Artist: Kerry Arquette

Fabric-Wrapped Beaded Bracelet

"It might tickle your wrist, but it also tickles your fancy," says artist Kerry Arquette. Polymer clay skull beads, created as shown on page 35, were used on this bracelet. In addition, round clay beads were covered with Day of the Dead fabric adhered to the beads with decoupage medium. Once dry, all the beads were strung on a piece of memory wire (wire that maintains its coiled shape). Feathery fiber was wound around the wire between beads.

Artist: Kerry Arquette

Artist: Kerry Arquette

Skeleton Fabric Brooch

"The small skeleton motifs on this fabric were perfect for my heritage brooch," says artist Kerry Arquette. Layers of Day of the Dead fabric were cut into rough petal shapes and dipped into fabric stiffener before being layered on a baked circular polymer base. As the petals dried, they were coaxed into curved shapes. A cropped image adorns the center of the brooch. The pin on the back was attached with clear-drying craft glue, and the piece was finished with glitter.

TRY THIS

When purchasing Day of the Dead fabric for making jewelry, consider your design concept. Most jewelry projects work best with fabrics with smaller-scaled motifs, such as quilting fabric. Larger motifs often must be cut down to be size-appropriate for jewelry use. In doing so, you may lose the detail of its Day of the Dead theme.

Marigold and Skull Pendant

Rustically beautiful, this pendant glows with upbeat Day of the Dead flavor and shines with rich gold gilding. All parts of the piece are created with polymer clay. You'll accomplish the earthy effect by gently removing painted portions and gilding the newly exposed sections. Tiny skulls peer out from beneath petals and from the flower's center, reinforcing the Day of the Dead theme.

 **Supplies**

- 4 ounces polymer clay
- Clay sculpting tools
- Narrow dowel
- Acrylic paints
- Paintbrush
- Water
- Bowl or sink
- Soft-bristled brush
- Gold gilding pen
- Black permanent marker
- Colored cords

 **Try This**

Most artists prime their baked polymer-clay creations with a coat of neutral-colored paint before moving forward with their project. But some projects, such as this necklace, benefit from some of the natural clay color remaining exposed. Polymer clay comes in a wide range of colors. Consider using a clay color complementary to your project so you can leave some areas exposed.

Artist: Kerry Arquette

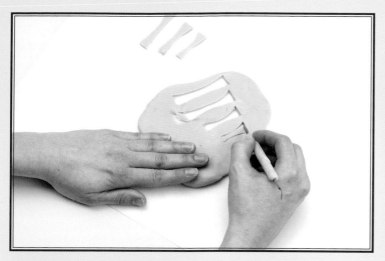

Step 1

To create the flower petals, roll or press a piece of clay into a thin sheet. Using a fine-tipped clay sculpting tool, cut rough, squared-off hour-glass shapes from the clay. Create four or five pairs of different petal sizes, ranging from approximately ¾" to 2".

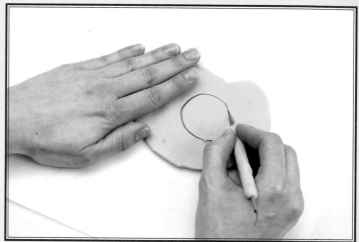

Step 2

To create the base of the pendant, roll or press a second piece of clay until it is approximately ¼" thick. Cut a 1" circle from the clay.

Step 3

Beginning with the longest pieces, lay the cut petal shapes across the circular base, overlapping in the center and extending over the edges of the base.

Step 4

Press a narrow dowel through the center of the layered shapes to connect them. You will see the outside petal edges of the layered pieces lift as you do so.

Step 5

Use your fingers to gently tear the edges of the flower petals and to shape the petals to curve in and upward.

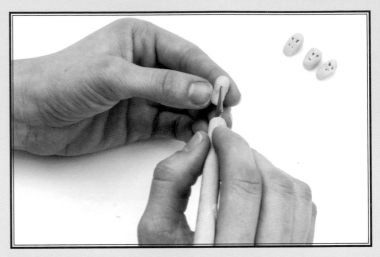

Step 6

Form small skulls from polymer clay, as shown on page 35. Use a fine-tipped clay tool to create eyes and noses.

Step 7

Gently press one of the skull shapes into the center of the flower. Tuck other skulls beneath the petals. Use a dowel to make a hole for hanging the pendant. Bake according to manufacturer's directions.

Step 8

Paint the pendant with three or four different colors of acrylic paints. Mix yellows, reds, and oranges. Allow to dry for approximately 20 minutes.

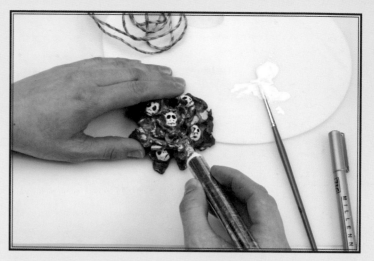

Step 9

Hold the painted pendant under water for a few minutes and remove. Gently wipe away small sections of paint with a soft-bristled brush. Allow to dry.

Step 10

Cover the newly exposed clay areas (those areas from which you removed paint) using a gold gilding pen. Paint the skulls white and detail their faces with a black marker. Hang the pendant from multiple strands of colored cords.

THE MEANING OF THE MARIGOLD

The marigold is the flower most associated with the Day of the Dead. It is called *cempoalxuchitl* (or *cempoalxochitl*), which means "20-flower." Some say the name relates to the sacred number 20 associated with early ritual calendars. Others believe it comes from the number of flower petals, or the number of years the perennial blooms. During Day of the Dead celebrations marigolds decorate altars and graves. Petals are sprinkled along pathways so spirits can be guided by the perfume. Petals are also used to create crosses on the ground in front of doorways. The belief is that as spirits pass over the cross while entering the house, any remaining sins will be eliminated. Because of their close association with the Day of the Dead, marigolds are one of the symbols that appear more frequently on Day of the Dead jewelry and other art.

Uncultured Pearl Earrings

Take a stroll through your local hobby store with the Day of the Dead foremost in your mind, and you're sure to see craft supplies in a completely different way. The uncultured pearls on these wonderful Day of the Dead earrings are a perfect example. The irregular shapes of the pearl beads, many with rounded "heads" and squared off "jaws," just scream, "SKULL!" Once faces were drawn on with a permanent marker, they were ready to string onto earrings.

 ## Supplies

- 6 uncultured pearl beads
- Permanent marker
- Decoupage medium
- Thin jewelry wire
- Jewelry pliers
- Wire cutters
- 10 small colored beads
- 2 earring pendants
- 2 earring wires

Artist: Kerry Arquette

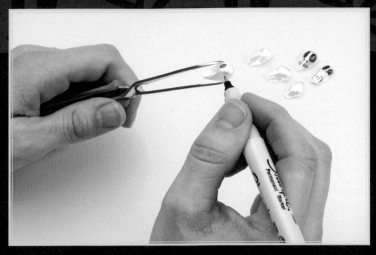

Step 1

Use a permanent marker to carefully draw faces on uncultured pearl beads. Seal the pearls with a coat of decoupage medium to prevent the marker from smearing off the slick surface.

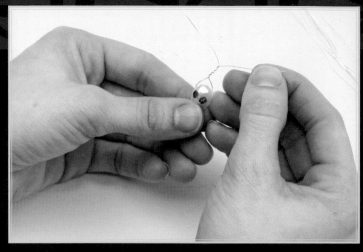

Step 2

Cut eight 4" pieces of slender jewelry wire. Slip a piece of wire halfway through the hole in one of the skull beads. Bring the two ends of the wire together above the bead. Cross the wire and twist several times to secure.

Step 3

Slide a bead onto the twisted wires directly above the skull bead. Slide the wires through a lower loop in the pendant. Twist the ends of the wires beneath the loop in the pendant until secure. Cut off the remaining wire. Repeat steps 2 and 3 to attach two more skull beads to the earring pendant.

Step 4

Slip one end of a piece of wire through the upper loop in the pendant. Cross the wires and twist, as you did in step 2. Slip two beads onto the twisted wires. Twist once again and form a loop. Use a jump ring to attach an earring wire to the pendant. Repeat steps 2-4 to make the matching earring.

Photo Transfer Necklace

At first glance, you'd swear that the skeleton beads on this striking necklace were carved out of stone, but they are actually carved from baked polymer clay. The image of the skull was transferred onto each piece and then baked into the clay. Turquoise and onyx beads were strung between the skulls, adding drama. Jade or coral also work well and will give your necklace a slightly different look.

Supplies

- 2-4 ounces white polymer clay
- Sculpting tools
- Liquid polymer clay
- Turquoise and onyx beads (or beads of your choice)
- Utility knife
- Spray varnish
- Jewelry wire
- Jewelry pliers
- Necklace clasp

Artist: Kerry Arquette

Step 1

Download skull images from the Internet and print them on a laserjet printer. Only laserjet prints will transfer. If you do not have a laserjet printer, make photocopies of your image. Print or photocopy two small, two medium, and two large images. Trim the individual images, leaving a small margin of white.

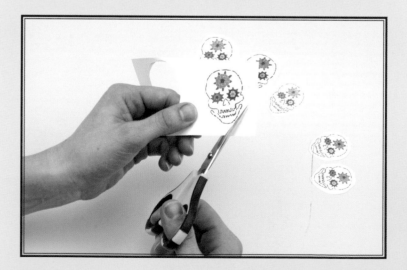

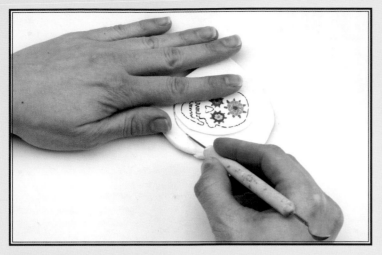

Step 2

Roll out a thin layer of white polymer clay. Place the skull images on the clay to use as a guide and carefully cut around the images. Gently remove any extra clay. Set aside the imagess.

Step 3

To create holes in the beads insert a thin piece of jewelry wire through each clay skull shape. You may leave the wire in place, or reinsert it after baking.

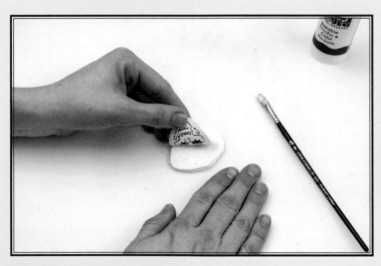

Step 4

Spread a thin layer of liquid polymer clay on the cut clay shapes. Gently press the skull images face-down on top of the liquid polymer clay. Burnish the image with your finger to remove any bubbles. Bake according to the manufacturer's directions.

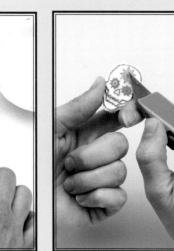

Step 5

Allow the baked clay shapes to cool. Soak them in water for a few minutes and peel off the paper. Finish by carving around the edges of the skull beads with a utility knife. Add small chips for a rustic effect. Spray with varnish to seal, and string the skull beads on a necklace wire with the other beads.

Artist: Jonathan Nicklow

Home Décor

Stunning decorations for your home

Forget mass-produced pieces of home décor or store-bought copies of paintings done by well-known artists. Decorate your place instead with Day of the Dead folk art you design and create! Two-dimensional Day of the Dead pieces can turn your home into a showpiece filled with quirky character. String a line of stunning papel picados, artfully cut paper banners, along the top of a wall for a unique border. Display painted glass depicting grinning calaveras in a window to catch the light. Use stickers and an old Grateful Dead record for a humorous clock project.

These two-dimensional home décor Day of the Dead pieces are perfect for adding a dash of color to white walls. They can be tamed and tuned down to work with a less flamboyant color palette. By modifying the designs, the projects can either be kitchy or classy.

Add to the presentation of your Day of the Dead two-dimensional home décor creations by placing vases of colorful marigolds on side tables. Throw a woven Mexican blanket over the back of a chair, and add a bright, hand-painted piece of pottery to a bookshelf.

Bring Your Home to Life

Day of the Dead art is the perfect way to bring interest to bare walls. Super-size your piece to fill a large expanse of wall space such as a hallway or the area over a fireplace, or modify the design so your project will fit neatly into a bare nook or cranny. Two-dimensional art can be functional as well as decorative. Make use of materials you already have to create many of these terrific projects.

Wooden Calaveras

"There is something to be said about the acknowledgment of death. It is not taboo. It should not be shunned and silenced," says artist Meagan Burns, whose fantastic wooden calaveras are so personable that it's impossible not to laugh out loud when looking at them. The prefabricated wooden forms are decorated with bits of fabric, beads, and other embellishments.

Meet the Artist: Meagan Burns

"I have lived in San Miguel de Allende, Guanajuato, Mexico, since early 2001. My first Halloween was spent at a cemetery in San Miguel de Allende, and I was absolutely amazed and moved by the respect for death that the Mexican culture demonstrates. The phrase 'Day of the Dead' is actually used *con mucho gusto*! Yes, death is sad, but to have a picnic on your grandmother's grave with music, delicious food, singing, and dancing…is there really any better way to celebrate the passing and pay tribute to the longing for a missed relative? Death will happen to each and every one of us, and how wonderful it is to know that there may be friends and relatives who serenade and make a festive toast to you. You may be there, you may not—we will not know until we have passed to the other side!"

Artist: Meagan Burns

Grateful Dead Clock

"You could make this fun clock using any old record, but I just couldn't help myself...I HAD to use an old Grateful Dead album!" says artist Kerry Arquette. The skeleton figures were created using printed copies of a clip-art skull. Image-editing software was used to flip the image. The skulls were cropped and then dressed in three-dimensional sticker outfits, which are available in most hobby stores. They were then mounted on painted chipboard circles and glued to the record. Clock numbers and mechanisms finish off the piece.

Artist: Kerry Arquette

Painted Shot/Juice Glasses

"What better way to celebrate Day of the Dead than with a toast to the departed?" asks artist Andrea Zocchi. These inexpensive glasses were painted with glass paint, available in most hobby stores. The skull patterns (on p 133) were taped to the inside of each glass. Using the pattern as a guide, paint was applied to the outside. Once complete, the paper pattern was removed and the glasses were baked according to manufacturer's directions.

Artist: Andrea Zocchi

DESIGN A PAPEL PICADO

Papel picados are decorative paper banners hung in doorways, across roads, and above altars during Day of the Dead celebrations. However, the banners' colorful and festive nature makes them the perfect decoration for any holiday, festivals, or celebration. Papel picados are described as a "take-away" craft because the design is created by removing negative space. What remains when you cut away portions of the paper is the final image. For this project, we use 8½ x 11" paper, but the size, colors, and theme of your papel picado are strictly up to you.

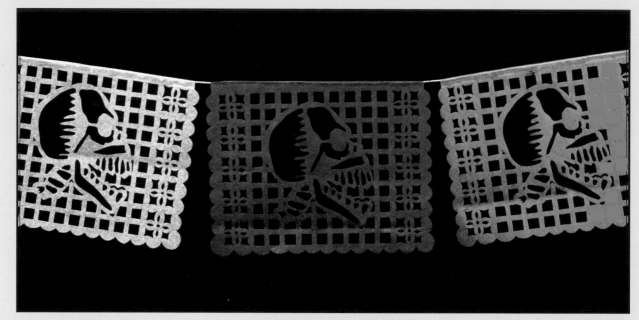

Artist: Jerry Vigil

 SUPPLIES

- Papel picado pattern page 140
- Tissue paper
- Stapler
- Craft knife and refill blades
- Staple remover
- Glue
- Paintbrush
- String

 TRY THIS

To easily spruce up your papel picados, use decorative-edge scissors to cut the tissue paper borders. There are many different styles of decorative scissors from which to choose, including scallops, hearts, zigzags, deckle, pinking, ripple, and corkscrew. When cutting delicate tissue, make sure your scissors are well-sharpened to avoid tearing.

Step 1

Enlarge or reduce the size of the papel picado template on page 140. Gather 10 to 12 sheets of tissue paper into a stack. (If your design is exceptionally complicated, you may wish to limit your stack to fewer pieces of tissue.) Center the design on top of the tissue paper and staple it at three points along the top edge.

Step 2

Begin cutting the shapes. For smooth cuts, maintain constant contact between the blade and the paper, and rotate the paper as you work.

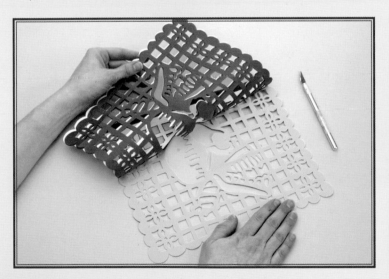

Step 3

Remove the staples and separate the sheets of tissue paper.

Step 4

Crease the top edge of one of the papel picados and apply white glue along the crease. Lay a length of string in the crease, leaving 4-6" of string exposed on either side of the tissue. Press the flap over and allow it to dry. Repeat for each banner. Tie the exposed strings together.

Papel Picado Lampshade

Papel picado is an excellent way to brighten up your living space. Colorful shades of paper are eye-catching, and the delicate nature of tissue softens an environment. Be traditional and string up a line of papel picados across a room or over a doorway, or use your favorite papel picado on a lampshade. Squared, rather than rounded, lampshades are easiest to work with. Use the same design on all four sides of the shade, or create a distinct design for each.

 ## Supplies

- Papel picado pattern page 141
- Sheet of plain white 8½ x 11" paper
- Sheet of 8½ x 11" graph paper
- Pencil
- Ruler
- Scissors
- Tissue paper
- Stapler
- Craft knife and extra blades
- Four-sided lampshade
- Craft paint
- Spray adhesive
- Clear-drying craft glue
- Embellishments

 ## Try This

Take the time to pick an effective color combination. When choosing paint for the lampshade, avoid picking dark colors that will keep the light bulb from illuminating the papel picado design. Take the tissue paper you plan to use with you when purchasing the paint for the shade. This will make it easier to make sure all the colors used in the project will work together.

Artist: Jerry Vigil

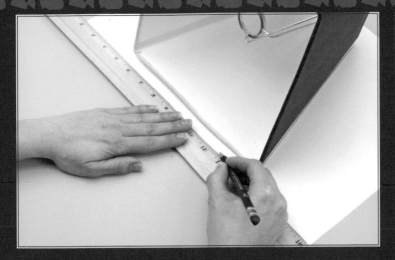

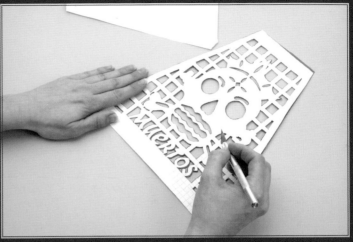

Step 1

Paint the sides of a lampshade. Create a template by tracing around one side of the lampshade onto a plain piece of paper. Leave a ½" border at the top and bottom of the traced template. Cut out the template.

Step 2

Size and photocopy your papel picado pattern so it fits within the boundaries of your template. Cut the pattern into the template shape. Place the pattern on four pieces of tissue and proceed to create your papel picados as directed on page 111.

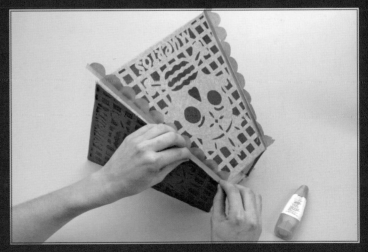

Step 3

Spray low-tack adhesive on one panel of the lampshade. Gently lay the papel picado on the lampshade panel so that the ½" margins overhang the top and bottom of the shade. Apply clear-drying craft glue to the insides of the border and fold it over. Repeat for the other panels.

Step 4

Embellish as desired. On this lamp, extra tissue paper was used to create a scalloped edge from top to bottom, but you could also use beads, baubles, and bells.

Day of the Dead Printmaking

Notecards, stationery, and invitations all beg for a process that creates multiple artistic handmade images. Printmaking is the ideal medium to achieve this goal. We are not talking about the sterile identical prints of a computer printer, but the rich and unique process of real ink on thick textured paper. In the process illustrated below, you will learn how to make a linoleum block print that is so wonderful you may wish to hang it on your wall.

Supplies

- Pencil
- Paper
- Linoleum block
- Transfer paper
- Linoleum carving tools (straight knife, V-shaped tools, and U-shaped gouges)
- Block-printing ink
- Smooth surface for ink (Glass or an old cookie tray will work)
- Brayer
- Porous heavyweight paper
- Spoon for burnishing

Artist: Matt Ritchie

Step 1

Sketch a simple, bold, high-contrast design on a piece of paper. Note that your print will mirror the design, so text will read backward. Once you are satisfied with your design, sketch it directly onto the linoleum block. Or, apply the image to the block by tracing over transfer paper.

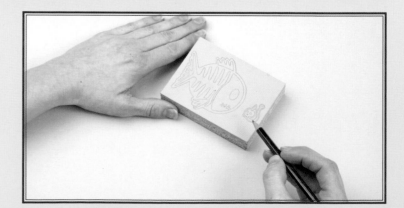

Step 2

Using linoleum-carving tools, begin to carve by removing the negative space. Do not carve too deeply, take away only the surface.

Step 3

Squeeze a small amount of block-printing ink onto a smooth surface, such as glass. Brayer the ink into a thin, smooth layer. Use the brayer to roll just enough ink onto the carved linoleum block to cover the positive spaces.

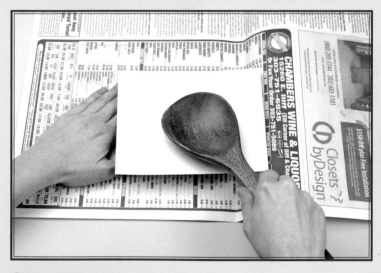

Step 4

Place your paper on the inked block. Once in place, be careful not to allow the paper to shift. Use a large spoon to gently burnish the paper.

Step 5

Gently peel the paper off the block and allow it to dry.

STUDENTS' INTERPRETATIONS

Introducing children to the Day of the Dead helps them build a healthy relationship with death and honor the lives of those who have passed. At West Middle School in Greenwood Village, Colorado, art teachers Justine Sawyer and Cindy Migliaccio asked students to research customs associated with the Day of the Dead and draw comparisons with Halloween and Memorial Day. Students then used lino print techniques to create these sophisticated and very imaginative lino prints.

Day of the Dead Pirate

"This is my favorite piece of artwork that I made this year," says artist Brandt Nelson. For him, the assignment conjured images of pirates. To create this duo-tone print, the design was sketched on paper and transferred to a rubber block. Lines assigned to the first ink color were carved away. The block was inked and pressed to the paper. Additional lines were removed before the block was inked with the second color. Once again, the block was pressed to the paper, adding to the original print. All the prints on theses two pages use this method.

Artist: Brandt Nelson

PRINTMAKING FUN FACTS

- In printmaking, each print is considered an original because it is not a reproduction of another piece of work.
- Prints created from one block are called an edition.
- The technique is an indirect transfer process because you apply the ink to the block and then create the print by pressing the block onto paper rather than directly applying ink to the paper.
- Prints are considered impressions because the inked block presses its mark into the paper.
- The prints shown on these pages are relief prints. Relief prints are made when ink is picked up by the positive space that is left from a carved surface. The negative image is left ink-free, and the resulting design is high-contrast.

Skeleton Scholar

"Only the educated are free," says artist Ryan Barney. That's the message behind his remarkable Day of the Dead block print. He believes that learning should continue beyond the grave in order for us to accomplish our full potential.

Artist: Ryan Barney

Artist: Madison Root

The Haunted Musician

"I play the guitar, which was my inspiration," says artist Madison Root. "He looks like me as a beginner." The cut image shows an excited, yet apprehensive, player on a stage. The lines in the background add movement to the piece, and the repeated music notes along the border add a real sense of visual rhythm.

PUZZLE-PIECED COMPOSITION

Wooden blocks are a staple of childhood, but they also can be used to create a stunning work of art. You can paint the blocks or cover them with decorative papers and piece them together like a beautiful puzzle. For the piece shown here, texture is the secret ingredient—the blocks and dowels used were covered with complementary textured papers and Day of the Dead artwork for a look that is bold and intricate.

SUPPLIES

- Pine board 17 x 18½"
- Saw
- Black acrylic paint
- Copies of Day of the Dead artwork printed in a variety of sizes
- Clear-drying adhesive
- Scissors
- Wooden pieces (Approx. measurements. All pieces are ½" thick.)
  (5) 5½ x 3" blocks
  (3) 3 x 3" blocks
  (1) 1½ x 3" block
  (6) 5½" square dowels
  (4) 3" square dowels
  (3) 5½" round dowels
- Textured decorative papers
- Heavy-duty adhesive
- Hanging hardware

Artist: Kerry Arquette

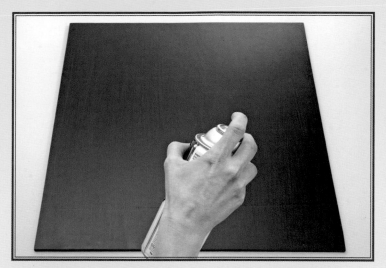

Step 1

Cut your piece of board to size. Any inexpensive and relatively sturdy type of wood will do. Paint the board black and allow to dry.

Step 2

Trim papers and artwork to fit your wooden blocks and dowels. Wrap papers around the blocks and dowels, gluing them on the back.

Step 3

Cut several of your images into pieces. Adhere them to a series of blocks that will be positioned side by side.

Step 4

Arrange the paper-covered blocks and dowels on your work surface as they will be placed when glued to the board. Adhere all of the blocks to the board using heavy-duty adhesive. Allow ¼" of space between each block so that the black board will be visible. When dry, attach the hanging hardware to the back of the piece.

WALL-MOUNTED CANDLEHOLDER

Embossed craft metal can be used to create the illusion of silver on your Day of the Dead pieces. The metal is pliable and easy to imprint with a stylus. Use the pattern on p 134, or create one of your own. You may need to back the metal, after cutting it, with a piece of cardstock or foam core to give it support. Paint the embossed piece, or buff it to a high sheen. Attach it to a colorful shelf, and then set a glowing votive in a glass votive candleholder in front. The metal will dance with each flicker, creating a delightful ambiance.

Artist: Andrea Zocchi

 SUPPLIES

- Pattern
- Craft metal
- Chipboard
- Art metal
- Acrylic paints
- Paintbrushes
- Paper towels
- Rubber cement
- 12" of a ¾ x 3½" pine board (Note: This dimension of lumber is referred to as 1 x 4" pine stock.)
- 6 x 3" Rectangular wood plaque
- 3½" decorative molding
- Saw
- Sandpaper
- Tack cloth
- Acrylic primer (gesso)
- Stylus
- Scissors
- Multipurpose craft glue
- Hanging hardware

Step 1

Photocopy the pattern on page 134. Cut out the skull shape.

Step 2

Trace the skull shape onto chipboard and cut it out.

Step 3

Place the chipboard template on a piece of craft metal. Use a stylus to trace around the template, and use scissors to cut out the metal shape.

Step 4

Use rubber cement to adhere the metal shape to the chipboard template. Place the original image on top of the metal shape, and use a stylus to trace the skull's features, creating an embossed metal skull.

Step 5

Apply a dark acrylic paint to the crevices of the embossed metal skull.

Step 6

Wipe off excess paint, leaving enough in the embossed areas to define the detail.

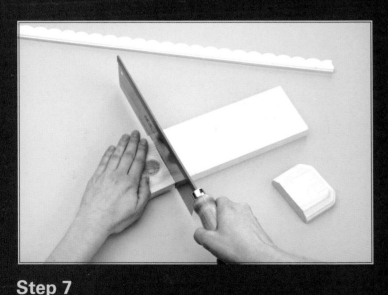

Step 7

Cut a piece of board into a 9" length. Cut a 3½" piece of decorative molding. Cut a store-bought wooden rectangle in half.

Step 8

Sand all wood pieces and use tack cloth to remove dust.

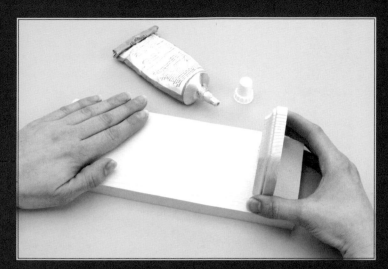

Step 9

Use multipurpose craft glue to adhere the wooden pieces together. Allow to dry.

Step 10

Use an acrylic primer such as gesso to paint the wood. After it's dry, apply blue paint. While the piece is still wet, use a paper towel to wipe off as much paint as you desire to give the piece a distressed appearance.

Step 11

Paint on details with acrylic paint. Seal with polyurethane.

Step 12

Use multipurpose craft glue to attach the embossed metal skull to the finished wooden candleholder. Apply hanging hardware.

CREATING WITH PUFF PAINT

Puff paint is a wonderful medium for Day of the Dead crafts. It's fun, easy to use, and available in many vibrant colors. Incorporating puff paint in the design adds dimension. Puff paint contains a glue-like binding agent that causes it to adhere to a variety of surfaces.

SUPPLIES

- Pattern
- Scissors
- Pencil
- 12" x 16" primed canvas paper
- Ruler
- Stencils
- Acrylic paint
- Paintbrushes
- Puff paints

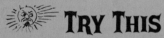

TRY THIS

Use stencils to ensure symmetry when decorating your skull. Place the stencil on the canvas. Trace around it. Flip the stencil over and reposition it on the opposite side of the skull's face. Trace. Repeat with other stencils, as desired.

Selma

"This painting is a tribute to my great-grandmother, Selma Margaret (Hulse) Ruther," artist Justine Sawyer says. "Great-Grandma Selma was an incredible woman who enjoyed life to the fullest each day, working hard while humming familiar tunes." To honor her subject, Justine chose a vibrant mix of colors and a whimsical design. The glittery puff paint details add just a hint of frivolity. To create the piece, Justine sketched a design using her own handmade stencils.

Artist: Justine Sawyer

Step 1

Photocopy the pattern on page 135. Cut it out and place it on your canvas paper. Trace around the pattern with a pencil. Use a ruler to draw a 2" frame around your skull. Use stencils, or freehand draw designs on the skull and frame. Leave minimal amount of negative space.

Step 2

Begin painting the skull with acrylic paint. Mix your own colors to create a unique color palette. Select mainly warm colors (red, orange, yellow, and their derivatives) or cool colors (blue, green, violet, and their derivatives). Use accents of the opposite color palette for contrast. Try to place contrasting colors next to one another for dynamic visual impact. Allow to dry.

Step 3

Use a variety of colors of fabric puff paint to accent designs with dots and lines. Practice with the puff paints on a scrap piece of paper to develop control of the material. Use glitter puff paints to add emphasis to focal points within the artwork. Try overlapping colors with a variety of dot sizes. (Allow to dry between applications.)

FROM THE ARTIST: JUSTINE SAWYER

"I have always been drawn to the vibrant artwork associated with the traditions surrounding the Day of the Dead. The dynamic colors and personal meaning behind the art make the work incredibly interesting. As preparation for teaching a unit based on the Day of the Dead for my middle school art students, I created this painting to share with my classes. It memorializes my great-grandmother, Selma. She quilted, crocheted, or baked each day, made her own lye soap, and walked everywhere in her Energizer pumps. Since her passing in 1984, my thoughts of her are still very frequent."

COLORFUL PUFF-PAINT CREATIONS

Puff paint is a type of fabric paint that, when applied, adds dimension to designs. It comes in a squeeze bottle with a pen-applicator tip, making it a great medium for children's art projects. The pieces shown here were created by students at West Middle School in Greenwood Village, Colorado. Art teachers Justine Sawyer and Cindy Migliaccio asked students to pay tribute to a person of their choice. The patterns and color schemes are reflective of the person chosen.

Dr. Martin Luther King Jr.

"This piece was created to honor Dr. Martin Luther King Jr.," says artist Emily Whaler. "I was inspired by his actions and ability to effect change." She placed flowers in the eyes of her skeleton to symbolize a bright and growing future despite King's passing.

Artist: Emily Whaler

Artist: Samantha Kagan

Elvis

"I tried to capture Elvis' creativity and musicality in this piece," says artist Samantha Kagan. On the background, she printed lyrics and song titles, and she incorporated musical staffs and notes into the facial design. Elvis' signature pompadour hairstyle tops off the piece.

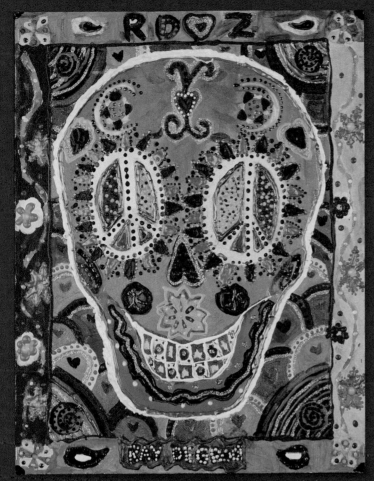

Artist: Charlotte Degroot

Ray

"Uncle Ray: The uncle any kid would want." That is how artist Charlotte Degroot describes this tribute to her treasured Uncle Ray. "He had such a colorful personality," she says. "He was a peaceful person with a wacky personality." These attributes led Charlotte to choose peace symbols for the eyes and an arsenal of color. She sketched her design on canvas, painted it with acrylic paint, and added details with puff paint.

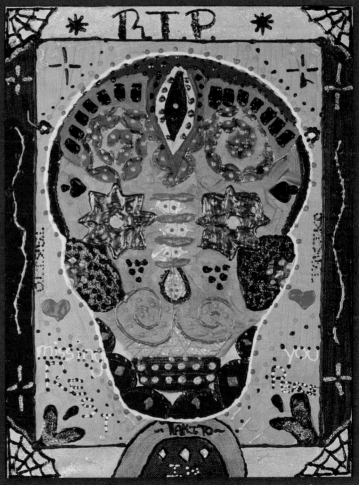

Artist: Amber Arenas

El Día de Takito

"This painting was inspired by the recent death of my puppy," says artist Amber Arenas. "I decided to dedicate the painting to Takito because he was with me all the time. The color scheme was inspired by his leash." The rest of the painting contains sweet offerings to Takito, such as flowers and lots of green grass for frolicking.

PAINTING ON GLASS

Glass is a wonderful canvas for Day of the Dead art. When hung in a window, the painted design casts jewel colors on nearby walls and furniture. Easy-to-use glass paints are available in most hobby stores. They can be applied to your glass with a brush or cotton swabs. Some paints also come in marker form. Many glass paints are baked in an oven to set the colors. Use glass paints to create Day of the Dead glasses for toasting the holiday!

 **SUPPLIES**

- Glass and frame
- Enlarged Day of the Dead artwork
- Masking tape
- Black glass paint pen
- Glass paints
- Paintbrushes and cotton swabs
- Embellishments
- Craft glue

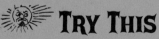 **TRY THIS**

Create a more complex piece of artwork by combining several Day of the Dead images on one piece of glass. Tape all your images to the back of your piece of glass. Use your black paint to create frames around the images and coordinate colors so the pieces support each other.

Artist: Kerry Arquette

Step 1

Choose a piece of artwork to reproduce on glass. Look for a simple image with distinct, bold lines, which will make this project easier to complete. Enlarge the piece to the desired size and print the image. Tape the image face-up to the back of the glass.

Step 2

Trace the image with a black glass paint pen.

Step 3

Fill in the borders of the image with colorful glass paints. Remove the paper from the glass. Bake, if required by the paint manufacturer. Cool.

Step 4

Embellish the picture frame. Apply hanging hardware.

Building Skeleton Puppets

Pinocchio, Lambchop, the Muppets. Irresistible? You bet. As are so many of the puppets that populated our childhoods. But there is no reason to leave puppets behind when you can make decorative, grown-up versions that celebrate the Day of the Dead. Give them as party favors to guests who are sharing your celebrations. Or, create a group of them to display in a vase as you would a bouquet of flowers. This puppet is pretty enough to enjoy and sturdy enough to play with, so feel free to share it with your favorite older child.

Supplies

- Pattern
- Heavy cardstock
- Craft knife
- Black marker
- Drill and drill bits
- Carbon/transfer paper
- Mini brads
- Dowel
- (2) ½" square wooden blocks
- Acrylic paint and colored pencils
- Paintbrush
- Multipurpose craft glue

Try This

In the pattern on page 136, we've included extra tabs in the arms and thigh bones. Drill holes where indicated to animate the puppet. To do so, tie a piece of string across the puppet's back to connect arm-to-arm. Do the same to connect legs. Tie a long piece of string to the middle of the "arm string." Extend it down the puppet's back and tie it to the "leg string." Allow remaining string to drape below the puppet. Move the arms and legs by pulling on the string.

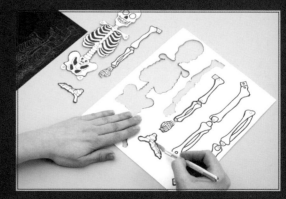

Step 1

Use carbon/transfer paper to transfer the pattern on page 136 onto heavy cardstock. Cut out the pieces with a craft knife.

Artist: Jerry Vigil

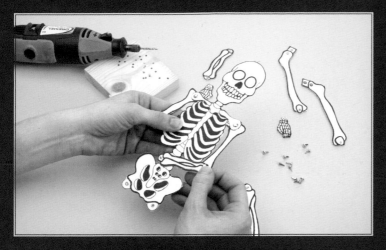

Step 2

Drill holes at the joints where indicated by circles. (We've included an extra set of circles in the tabs of the arm and thigh bones to animate the puppet, should you wish. See the instructions in the Try This box on the opposite page.) Insert mini brads through the circles to connect the joints. Work the joints until they move easily.

Step 3

Drill holes for your dowel in the center of two small blocks of scrap wood. Run the dowel through the drilled holes.

Step 4

Use acrylic paints, colored pencils, or markers to decorate the puppet as desired.

Step 5

Use multipurpose craft glue to prevent the dowels from slipping within the blocks. Use multipurpose craft glue to attach the blocks to the back of your puppet.

PATTERNS

Drawing a skull, skeleton, papel picado, or complex Day of the Dead design is easy when you have a pattern. Photocopy the pattern of your choice. Enlarge or decrease the size as you wish. Cut out the pattern and trace around it, or use a light box, carbon/transfer paper, or graph paper to transfer the image to your work surface. If you wish, use the pattern for inspiration and freehand draw the design directly onto your artwork.

Ornate Skulls

More ornament usually means more detail. Giving a skull more detail can either emphasize the ominous nature of a skull or bring out the whimsy in the design.

Artist: Andrea Zocchi

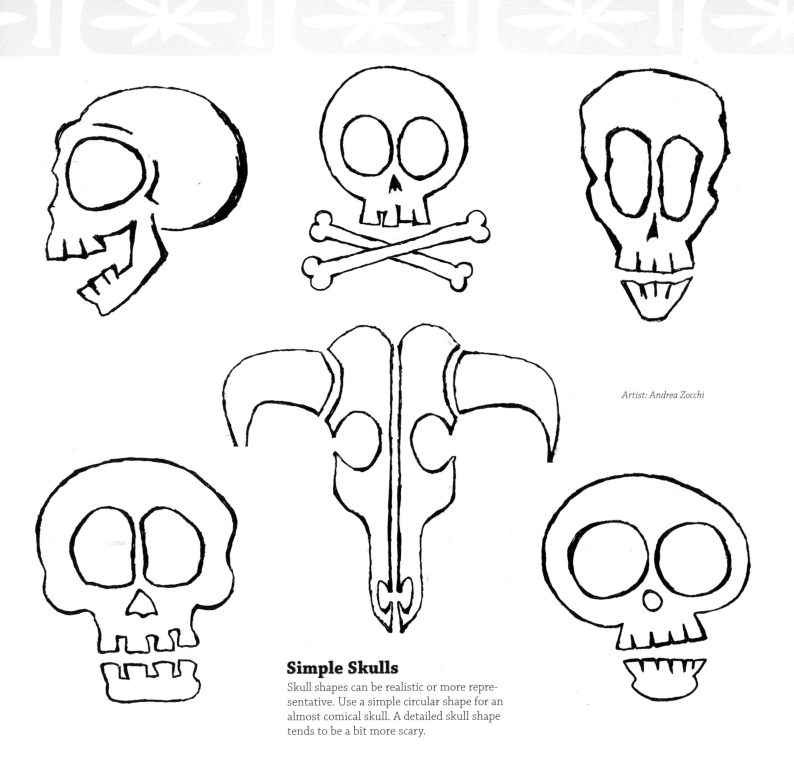

Artist: Andrea Zocchi

Simple Skulls

Skull shapes can be realistic or more representative. Use a simple circular shape for an almost comical skull. A detailed skull shape tends to be a bit more scary.

Patterns for Candleholder

Artist: Andrea Zocchi

Embossed Candleholder, P 120

The embossed metal candleholder utilized this terrific design. Trace it as directed in the instructions, or get fancy by transferring it to a T-shirt and painting the design with fabric paints.

Bones and Vines

This organic pattern can be used in a variety of projects including the candleholder on page 120. It would also work well as a painting on glass.

Artist: Andrea Zocchi

PATTERN FOR PUFF PAINT

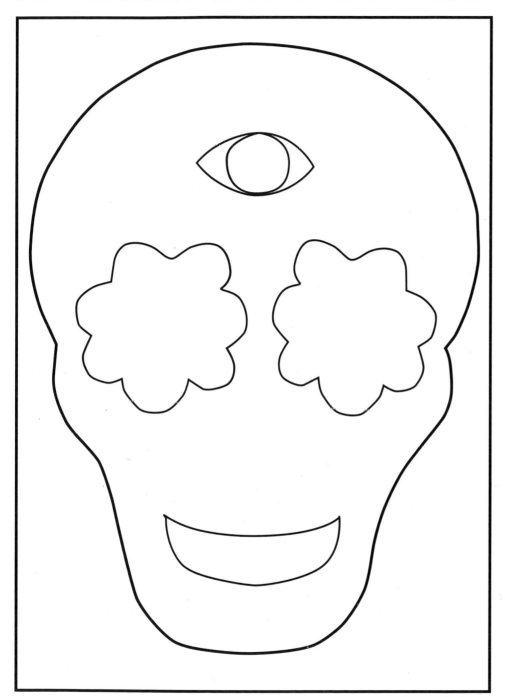

Artist: Justine Sawyer

Puff Paint on Canvas, P 124

The puff paint on canvas project was made using this template. Cut it out and place it on your canvas. Trace the template. By adding simple shapes, like those below, you can customize your painting.

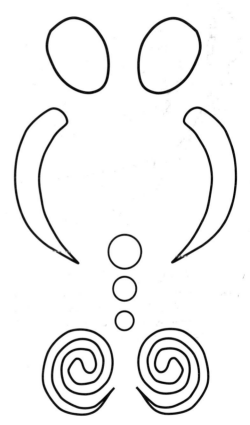

DOLL AND PUPPET PATTERNS

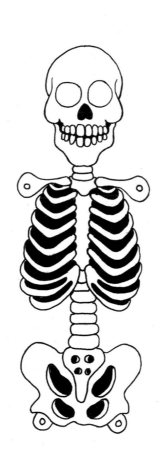

Artist: Andrea Zocchi

Skeletons in My Closet Paper Doll, P 52

Cut out this pattern. Trace it onto black cardstock to create the skeletons for your own "calaveras in the closet" project.

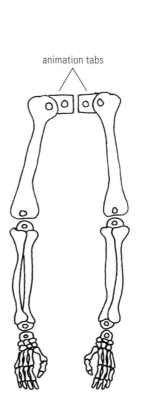

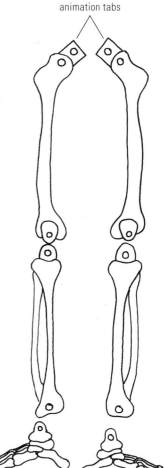

animation tabs

animation tabs

Artist: Jerry Vigil

Stick Puppet Pattern, P 130

Use this pattern to create the body, arms, and legs for your stick puppet. Enlarge or minimize the pieces to create an entire calavera puppet family. The square tabs at the ends of the arms and legs are included for mobilizing the puppet, should you wish. Instructions for mobilization appear in the Try This box on page 130.

LINO PRINT PATTERNS

Lino Drawings, P 114

Make your own lino print fish calavera cards or wall art using this terrific pattern. Or use one of the additional patterns seen here. Try printing on paper, fabric, or even wood!

Artist: Matt Ritchie

Papel Picado Patterns

Use these patterns to create wonderful papel picado banners and lampshades. Mix up the designs for a more dramatic and visually interesting effect.

Artist: Jerry Vigil

Artist: Jerry Vigil

Papel Picado Pattern, P 110

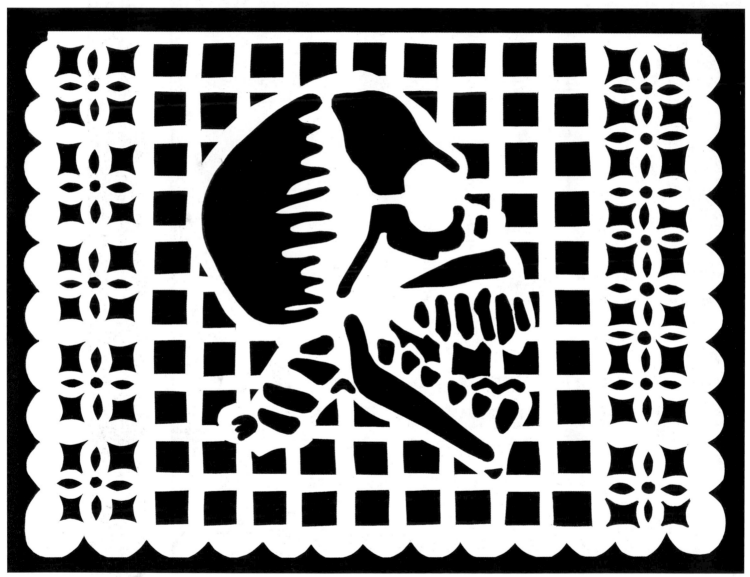

Artist: Jerry Vigil

Papel Picado Lampshade Pattern, P 112

Artist: Jerry Vigil

RESOURCES

Day of the Dead References

- AZ Central - Arizona tourism site with Day of the Dead information, www.azcentral.com/ent/dead

- Calle Olvera - Resource for Olvera Street, includes links, photos, art workshops, and more, www.calleolvera.com

- Day of the Dead in Mexico - Author, Mary J. Andrade, online resource, www.dayofthedead.com

- Day of the Dead Folk Art Gallery - Depot for art, articles, and galleries, www.ddfolkart.com

- Día de los Muertos - Blog that revolves around the holiday, includes links, store, and lesson plans, www.diadelosmuertos.us

- Hollywood Forever Cemetery, Famous cemetery that is home to one of Los Angeles' Day of the Dead celebrations, www.hollywoodforever.com/hollywood/

- Mexico Connect - Articles, forums, information, and insight as related to Mexico, includes a database on history, tourism and more, www.mexconnect.com

- Oaxaca Live - Details Oaxaca, Mexico's most recognized celebration, www.oaxacalive.com/muertos.htm

- Olvera Street - Community Web site for the "birthplace of Los Angeles," which is also home to one of the most festive Day of the Dead celebrations in the United States, www.olvera-street.com

- Yucatan Today - Tourist and traveling site with great Day of the Dead traveling tips, www.yucatantoday.com

Where to Buy

- Casa Mexicana - Retailer of Mexican folk art, www.yucatantoday.com

- Etsy.com – Online market for handmade goods, just type "Day of the Dead" into the search field to find artists

- Folk Tree - Retailer of Mexican folk art, 217 South Fair Oaks, Pasadena, CA 91105, (626) 795.8733, www.folktree.com

- Santa Fe Pottery - Retailer of Mexican folk art, 323 S Guadalupe St., Santa Fe, NM 87501, (505) 989-3363, http://www.santafepottery.com/

- Silver Crow Creations - Online depot for Day of the Dead shrines, nichos, and calaveras, www.silvercrowcreations.com

- Tu Pueblo Imports - Wholesale Mexican folk art and tutorials, www.tupuebloimports.com

Olvera Street, Los Angeles

Galleries

- Lakewood Cultural Center, 470 South Allison Parkway, Lakewood, CO 80226, (303) 987.7876, www.lakewood.org

- Lawndale Art Center, 4912 Main Street, Houston, TX 77002, (713) 528.5858, www.lawndaleartcenter.org

- Milagros Mexican Folk Art Gallery, www.milagrosgallery.com, (877) 939.0834

- Pico House Gallery At El Pueblo Historical Monument, 424 North Main Street, Los Angeles, CA 90012, (213) 485.6855, www.lacity.org/elp

- Self Help Graphics - 3802 Cesar E. Chavez Avenue, Los Angeles, CA 90063, (323) 881.6444, www.selfhelpgraphics.com

Events

- Los Angeles, California
  November 1 – 2, Hollywood Forever Cemetery, www.ladayofthedead.com

  Late October, Festival de la Gente, 6th Street Bridge, Whittier Boulevard and S. Boyle Avenue

- Petaluma, California
  For a listing of events, visit, www.petalumaartscouncil.org

- Phoenix, Arizona
  For a listing of events, visit www.azcentral.com/ent/dead

- San Francisco, California
  November 1 – 2, Mission District, San Francisco, California,
  www.dayofthedeadsf.org

- NYC, New York
  For a listing of events, visit,
  http://www.elmuseo.org/diadelosmuertos/Calendar_Of_Events.html

Artists' Web Sites

- Denise Alvarado, www.mysticvoodoo.com
- Kerry Arquette, www.cantatabooks.com, www.thechicksguide.org
- Meagan Burns, www.ondaroja.com
- Jodi Cain, www.tatteredrags.net
- Cesco (Frank Pamies), www.cesco.etsy.com
- Ofelia Esparza, www.ofeliaesparza.com
- Erikia Ghumm, www.erikiaghumm.com
- Kari Hansen, www.greenpear.com
- Karen Hickerson, www.karenhickerson.com
- Ramona Hotel, www.whohadada.org/ramonahotel
- Brandon Kihl, www.kihlstudios.com
- Tamra Kohl, www.claylindo.com
- Matt Ritchie, http://matt136.deviantart.com
- Michelle Ritchie, http://alteredboxes.deviantart.com
- Jenn Rodriguez, www.qrow.com
- Jerry Vigil, www.vigilarte.net
- Andrea Zocchi, www.cantatabooks.com, www.thechicksguide.org

Clip Art

Lee Hansen
http://www.leehansen.com

Model

Erin Mahrer, The Chick's Guide Agency, www.thechicksguide.org

Chapter Opener Art Descriptions

P 28 Aztec Warrior Calavera, by Jerry Vigil

An Aztec warrior is depicted in this complex polymer clay calavera. The calavera's blue face, one of the artist's trademarks, is surrounded by a ferocious leopard mask. The warrior's body is painted with a leopard print. Brightly colored beads add flame to the tawny color palette.

P 58 Puff Paint Mask, by Pam Hauer

This paper mache mask was painted with white acrylic and then decorated with patterned papers and puff paint. Clip art images were cropped to fit in the center of the eyes.

P 80 Metal and Button Choker and Earrings, by Kerry Arquette

A piece of crunched craft mesh was stitched to a piece of wide black satin to form the base of this choker. Buttons, decoupaged with Day of the Dead images, were stitched to the mesh. The earrings were made by gluing mesh to buttons before being decoupaged with Day of the Dead images. The backs were clipped off of the buttons and earring posts were glued in their place.

P 106 Stitched Block Print, by Jonathan Nicklow

Block print designs were stamped onto earthy colored paper to create this wall decoration. Patterned papers, cut to form the borders of the artwork, were stitched in place with red embroidery thread. Block print sections were stitched together in a similar manner.

About the Authors

Kerry Arquette, first published at age thirteen, has work featured in *Seventeen, Good housekeeping, Ladies' Home Journal* and other popular magazines. She has authored more than a dozen books, including *Daddy Promises* and her award-winning children's picture book *What Did You Do Today?* She is a cofounder of Cantata Books Inc.

Andrea Zocchi, cofounder of Cantata Books, Inc., was an art director for a large design and how-to book and magazine publisher. Multitalented and versatile, he has worked as a graphic designer, freelance photogrpher, director of a foreign studies program, sales manager, and farmhand.

Jerry Vigil, a self-taught Chicano artist, has carved bultos and retablos since 1998. Known in his hometown of Denver as the "Dean of the Dead," he is a high-profile art activist and instructor whose work has appeared in dozens of local and national exhibits and competitions as well as numerous publications. His signature calaveras are a distinctly vibrant blue.

INDEX